DUST

UNIVERSITY OF CALIFORNIA PRESS *berkeley los angeles london*

A HISTORY OF THE SMALL AND THE INVISIBLE $DUST$

Joseph A. Amato

University of California Press
Berkeley and Los Angeles, California

University of California Press, Ltd.
London, England

Library of Congress Cataloging-in-Publication Data

Amato, Joseph Anthony.
    Dust : a history of the small and the invisible / Joseph A. Amato.
        p.   cm.
    Includes bibliographical references.
    ISBN 0-520-21875-2 (alk. paper).
    1. Dust—Social aspects—History.   2. Size perception.   3. Science—
Philosophy.   I. Title.
RA577.D8 A48   2000
551.51′13—dc21   99-27115

Manufactured in the United States of America

08   07   06   05   04   03   02   01   00   99
10   9   8   7   6   5   4   3   2   1

To my father,
Joseph Amato (1912–1989)

CONTENTS

FOREWORD
JEFFREY BURTON RUSSELL

What is dust? We all know what it looks like, especially when it forms dust mice under the bed. But what in fact is it? One way to answer is the scientifically mechanical. Unlike such exotic dusts as interstellar particles, ordinary house dust is a mixture of dead insect parts, flakes of human skin, shreds of fabric, and other unpleasing materials. House dust is a medical problem because it is the home of whole populations of microscopic dust mites, which eat human skin particles, excrete twenty times a day, and produce a new generation every three weeks. Millions of people in the United States alone suffer severe allergic reactions to mite excreta and thus to dust. When house dust is contaminated by substantial quantities of animal and human excreta, it becomes infectious and is often called "dirt." As dirt, dust becomes a vector of disease and a severe health problem.

At this point the nature of dust becomes a historical and conceptual as well as a scientific question: we can investigate how people through the centuries have defined dust, reacted to it, tolerated it, attacked it, been defeated by it (as during the Dust Bowl), and even legislated against it. One answer to the conceptual question is that dust is what people have thought it to be through the centuries. That approach links the history of dust with the history of the minuscule, "the small and the invisible." Through vast stretches of time past, people have thought of dust as the smallest possible thing, leading to expressions such as "fine as dust" or "less than dust."

In this original and eloquent work of interdisciplinary synthesis, Joseph Amato melds his firm grasp of the history of concepts with social, medical, and political history; with the history of hygiene, public policy, and the natural sciences. All of Amato's work has shown this extraordinary combination of the finely philosophical (*Mounier and Maritain*, 1975) with the concrete and particular (*When Father and Son Conspire: A Minnesota Farm Murder*, 1988) and with personal and moral commitment (*Victims and Values*, 1992). *Dust* is the most richly synthetic book of all; it is both narrative and analytical, both a pleasure and a mind-opening experience. It is a personal, practical, psychological, and philosophical book.

The history of the concept of dust is essentially the history of the concept of the minute and minuscule. As such, it underwent an enormous transformation in the late nineteenth and twentieth centuries, when microscopes, electron microscopes, and particle accelerators demoted (or promoted) dust from the microcosmic to the mesocosmic. A grain of house dust is roughly halfway in size between a subatomic particle and the planet Earth. And the world of the subatomic meets with the world of the inconceivably vast in quantum mechanics, which the human mind can understand only mathematically.

The world in which we discuss quarks, neutrinos, DNA, and viruses is very different from the world people inhabited and envisioned before the nineteenth century. Then, the smallest thing known was dust itself, and dust was the commonest metaphor for anything of low status. Just as a Roman general riding in triumph always had a slave behind him repeating, "Remember, you are only a man," so Christians have been reminded yearly on Ash Wednesday, "Remember that you are dust and will return to dust." Everything on earth was corruptible; only the cosmos beyond the moon was immutable. And beyond the cosmological was the theological. What was the ultimate meaning of great and small? Was God great, or small, or both, or neither?

Beside the conceptual history of the minuscule is its cultural history. Is tininess good or bad? Is it to be praised or execrated, accepted or eradicated? Is dust dirt? Is dirt dangerous? Dirt and dust dominated the lives of people everywhere before the nineteenth century; in most places, they still do. More people—an estimated three billion—are living today without rudimentary hygiene than lived at any time in the past.

The tiny was a matter of wonderment from the time that Democritus and Lucretius speculated on the existence of atoms. In early European culture it was seen as the mysterious source of life (not only embryonically but in the sense that some life actually arose from the inanimate minuscule by spontaneous generation). It was also seen as a cause of death and disease. The claim that medieval and early modern people ignored hygiene is nonsense. But it is true that they did not understand what they were up against.

Only in the course of the nineteenth and early twentieth centuries did hygiene evolve from a ritual or a matter of comfort to a scientific system. With the discovery of the microscope came the discovery of the microbe and the mechanisms of disease transmission. Doctors and nurses began to wash their hands between patients. Housewives and housemaids mounted an ever more furious attack on dust, which had been clearly demonstrated as evil: it was dirt, the home of germs and the source of disease. Amato calls the period from the mid-nineteenth to the mid-twentieth century "the great cleanup." Dust and dirt became enemies that had to be controlled, both by individuals with vacuum sweepers and by governments with sewage systems and hygiene programs.

But the great cleanup has had two ironic aspects. The first is that technology, while producing more ways of controlling dust, has added enormously to the varieties and dangers of dust in such forms as radioactive particles, smog, and toxic chemicals. The second is that since the 1960s people living in advanced societies have increasingly and dangerously ignored the hard-won lessons of hygiene. Just as young Americans in the 1960s took wealth for granted, young Americans today are taking health for granted. But, as Amato makes clear, the war on dust and dirt has not brought a victory over disease.

For better and for worse, dust has had dramatic social, scientific, and, since 1945, even cosmic effects. It deserves a history. It has one here.

LITTLE THINGS MEAN A LOT

> Vast is the kingdom of dust! Unlike terrestrial kingdoms, it knows
> no limits. No ocean marks its boundaries. No mountains hem it in.
> No parallels of latitude and longitude define its boundless areas, nor
> can the farthermost stars in the infinitudes of space serve other than
> as a twinkling outpost of a realm as vast as the universe itself.
> —J. Gordon Ogden, *The Kingdom of Dust*

Mothered by the same earth, dust and dirt have different fathers. Dust—finer and more discrete—belongs as much to air as to earth. Dirt—bigger and clumsier—is identified with soil. When wet, dirt reveals a closer kinship to water than to dust. But dirt's real father, which vouches for its closer affinity to the soil, is muck or, to be more precise, excrement. This book is much more about dust than dirt; it is about dust's role as a condition of life and as a measure of the small until the start of this century.

Once, not so long ago, dust constituted the finest thing the human eye could see. In the form of gold dust or pollen, as light filaments that covered the skin, or as individual particles that spun in the sunlight, dust was the most minuscule thing people encountered. Like darkness and skin, dust was an omnipresent boundary, in this case between the visible

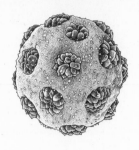

A grain of pollen

and the invisible. In advanced twentieth-century society, visible dust has been removed from the surface of most things, and the kingdom of dust has been opened to examination by scientific instruments. It has been studied, regulated in industry and society, and controlled in dwellings, in public buildings, and on the streets. Dust, always varied in composition, is now seen as a highly diverse particulate and a matter of submicroscopic exactness. Along with so many other minute things of the preindustrial world, dust has been swept to the edges of contemporary society and, thus, to the margins of contemporary consciousness.

As with all that was once considered really small, dust has been redefined by a great twentieth-century revolution—a revolution of the minuscule. Denied the intellectual fanfare of the astronomical revolution, which removed the earth from the center of the universe and declared the universe infinite, this revolution of the petite declared the infinity of the infinitesimal. It has forced humans to recognize the immensity and might of the small. For the first time ever, at least for those with inquisitive minds, the world below became as vast, fascinating, and powerful as the heavens above.

The roots of this revolution lie in early modern history, with the development of finely made human goods and the first microscopic perceptions of reality. It has been sustained with the discovery of microbes and the diagnosis and cure of viral and bacterial diseases; the reading of DNA and the deciphering of genes; and the division and fusion of atoms. Among its consequences was the end of the perennial identification of dust and smallness.

DUST: THE COMMON MEASURE

Throughout the ages, dust has been the first and most common measure of smallness. Dust is a result of the divisibility of matter.[1] Even the hardest materials erode and become dust. The ivory of piano keys and the coins of the realm become smooth and worn over time, adding themselves, bit by bit, to dust.[2] Softer materials abundantly supply the microscopic stuff that flows around the islands of perceptible and palpable objects. An average puff of a cigarette has been estimated to contain 4 billion particles of dust. The vapor that condenses on a dry plate—water dust, so to speak—is 500,000 times thinner than a sheet of writing paper. A grain of musk perfumes a room for years, and a single grain of indigo colors a ton of water.

Amorphous, dust is found within all things, solid, liquid, or vaporous. With the atmosphere, it forms the envelope that mediates the earth's interaction with the universe.[3] It flies over the highest mountains and crosses the widest seas. It fills the still air of home and the busy air of streets. It comes to rest everywhere in nature and on the human body. The finest dust—dust that can enter the pores of human skin— comes to rest in the oceans' depths. It falls with every drop of rain and flake of snow, and in the course of a year it can cover the rooftops of buildings with tons of fine debris. Even in the cleanest conditions, it has been estimated, "there are over a thousand motes of dust in every cubic inch of air."[4]

Dust is everywhere because its source is everything. Its most remote origins in time and space are the Big Bang, collapsing stars, and the dark line across the center of the Milky Way, which, according to astronomer Donald Brownlee, "is a line of dirt perhaps 65,200 light-years across, and 3.832×10^{17} miles long."[5] Here on earth, dust comes from everything under the sun: minerals, seeds, pollen, insects, molds, lichens, and even bacteria. Its sources also include bone, hair, hide, feather, skin, blood, and excrement. And things of human fabrication, too numerous to mention, also cover the earth and fill the atmosphere with dust.

Dust goes where the wind lists. As if it were nothing at all—without mass, without volume, the featherweight of featherweights—it rises up and forms a vapor and haze. Indeed, these qualities evoke its etymological origin in the German word *Dunst*, which means vapor.[6] Dust is as fine and familiar a thing as the unaided human eye can perceive.

While doubtless certain dusts are identified with precious metals and life-giving pollens (which themselves once were used to measure the smallest things), dust commonly travels with the children of earth: dirt, mud, and muck. Unnoticed, trodden underfoot, it is associated with the lowliest things, with what is broken, discarded, and formless. Although dust can be identified with the precious essence of things, its most regular associates are fragments, tailings, splinters, scraps, shreds, morsels, chips, and nicks. It is commonly identified with the trivial, meager, petty, scanty, puny, and picayune. For these reasons, dust would appear to be neither a subject worthy of reflection nor meritorious enough to serve a history of smallness.

Dust as an element cannot claim the glory of light, the subtlety of air, the solidity of earth, or the vitality of water, even though it envelops galaxies, circles planets, and hides in the bedrooms of kings and queens. Scattered throughout the atmosphere and the universe, its refracting power helps account for why and how humans see light itself. It explains blue skies and daylight, with the array of rich and diffuse colors we cherish. Dust's refracting power also explains why so little light—visible radiation—reaches the earth in its long trek from the sun.[7]

Dust forms the ceaseless tides of the becoming and dissolution of things. Out of it things are made; into it they dissolve. So constant, so pervasive, dust, aggregating and disintegrating, gauges matter on its way to and from being. So dust would seem to measure history and the historian, not the reverse.

Dusts are part of the earth's continual making and unmaking. Desert storms fill the skies for thousands of miles and change seasons, vegetation, and landscapes. Over centuries, blown dust accumulates into geological structures like the loess hills of Iowa and the cliffs of northwest China, composed of deposited dust from the Gobi Desert. These structures shape human life.

Volcanoes shower the earth with fine particles of dust. The largest volcanic eruptions have been estimated to affect ten thousand square miles of the earth and to form mushroom clouds that rise to the edge of the atmosphere. (The eruptions from Mount St. Helens shot up twelve miles into the sky.)[8] Volcanic dust, which has altered the entire world's climate by impeding sunlight and shortening growing seasons,

Dust storm

may have accounted for the ice ages. The weather of the year 1816, known in Scandinavia, Britain, and the United States as "the year without a summer," was the result of a volcanic eruption in Sumbawa, Indonesia.[9]

Even fires and explosions have made their mark in the history of dust. The Chicago Fire of 1871 poured such large quantities of ash into the sky that forty days afterward the cinders reached the Azores, in the middle of the North Atlantic.[10] The 1954 hydrogen bomb test in the Bikini Islands spread radioactive dust particles over seven thousand square miles. Surely, dust impinges on human history.

Dust also leaves human fingerprints on a landscape. To take the instance with which contemporary North Americans are most familiar, dust imprinted the "Dirty Thirties." From 1932 to 1938, the so-called

Dust Bowl covered 150,000 square miles of the American plains, causing 60 percent of the people there to emigrate.[11] No history of the American Midwest in the 1930s fails to mention dust-darkened skies, dust-filled ditches, dust turning day into night. Dust found its way into people's beds and food; it tore at their skin and caused "dust pneumonia." It colored—or darkened—the way people felt about life and themselves. However, the Dirty Thirties were about more than dry and dusty times. They were also about the consequences of expanded agriculture and unregulated grazing practices on the American central plains.[12] Each handful of dust judged a people's management of its land.

NEW DUSTS, NEW MEASURES

Human beings have been changing the earth and kicking up dust ever since their origin. Long ago, dust was the common measure of our work with things: it indicated how much, with what, and how finely we worked. We made dust when we dug, sawed, drilled, snapped, filed, crushed, ground, polished, pulverized, and milled. We made dust fly when we broke trails, laid foundations, erected structures, built roads, and laid tracks. Human engines—from early windmills to coal-burning steam engines to contemporary nuclear reactors—discharge dusts that determine the character of regions.

Though there is no etymological connection between the words *dust* and in*dust*ry, industrial societies created more, and more varied, dusts than had any previous society.[13] Armed with steel tools, dynamite, and bulldozers, industrial society transformed the earth, belching unprecedented amounts and varieties of dusts into the environment. For the sake of cotton irrigation in Kazakhstan and Uzbekistan, rivers were diverted from the Aral Sea, shrinking and salinizing the sea and producing a salt-filled dusty wind that caused lung ailments. By all previous measures, industrial society was the great earth mover and, consequently, the great dust maker.

Every industry creates a peculiar dust and smoke. Because of this, and because of climatic conditions, each industrial city had its own distinguishing haze and smog. The darkened skyline of turn-of-the-century Minneapolis grain mills was different from that painted by the steel foundries of Gary, Indiana. Contemporary Chicago's air pollution differs from that of Los Angeles, and the smog of Los Angeles is not the same as London's.[14]

Dusts vary by time as well as by activity and place. They both belong to and define distinct historical periods. The dusts of London under bombardment during World War II differed from the great London smogs of the postwar period. In the dusts of Auschwitz's crematoria historians detect a different moral accusation from the one they find in the radioactive dusts of Chernobyl.

Dusts, which contemporary sensibility is disposed to consider only as pollutants, also reveal a history of beneficial service to humans. To suggest just a few of many examples, dust has furnished rich minerals and supplemented soils. It has been used to make bricks, ceramics, and glass. It has provided chalk for writing, clay bases for cosmetics, talc for drying bodies, and a range of powders for such basic manufacturing processes as purification, grinding, desiccation, adhesion, aggregation, and pigmentation. Powdered peat runs trains in Sweden. Clays are used for a vast range of products.[15] Essential for agricultural and industrial processes and products, dusts also protect plants against cold and insects; they filter liquids. Dust can be both an essence of things and the best means of getting at the essence of other things.

Today society lives relatively free of visible dust. Indeed, some computer factories and laboratories are designed to be without a single particle of dust in them—and being free of dust has become a uniquely contemporary ideal. In the past, however, dust accompanied humans always and everywhere. Its invasions were as certain as the changing of the seasons. Starting in the nineteenth century, new industrial dusts (many of which were studied under microscopes) joined traditional dusts in home and street, defining much of the sight, feel, and smell of urban life. The quantity of dust increased with the hubbub of the cities. New dusts accompanied the steam engine, the locomotive, and the iron and steel industries when human beings chewed up the earth as never before. Coal and silicon dusts had a particular association with industry.

Yet it is not accidental that in nineteenth-century industrial society— in England first and foremost—dust was declared an enemy by public health officials. Sanitarians asserted a relationship between dust and disease. Industrial hygienists demonstrated that dusts caused a range of maladies among miners and other industrial workers.

The processes that caused so much dust and waste gave society the means and the desire to control them. By the last quarter of the nineteenth century, Western society had begun to sanitize and cleanse itself. It compounded this desire with a moral ideal of purity. Governments ordered delousing, pasteurizing, and sterilizing. They directed a range of ordinances against dusts, trash, noise, and, in the United States, whatever other material and moral turpitude could be trapped under the wide statutory net of "unwanted nuisances." In the same period, homes became the target of domestic cleaning manuals that advised women and servants how to protect home and family against dusts and other minuscule invaders. Different institutions advocated different cleaning regimens. The regime of the army barracks was not that of the public school, which in turn differed from those of the hospital and the factory. All dusts became defined targets of state and national health campaigns.

However, in most sectors of society, fighting dust made little headway until the 1930s and 1940s. Even though the switch from horses to automobiles, the paving of streets, and the seeding of lawns had already diminished dusts considerably, until then there simply were not enough tools and products to scour the environments where dirt and pests abounded. As remorseless as the tide, dust was thrown up by the churning of steam engines and tracked up and down streets and into buildings, and it made itself at home in the collection of ill-kept goods of everyday households.

While the public conquest of dust involved all of society and its new technologies, the battle against domestic dust was fought in the household trenches. Its instruments included an array of new cleaning devices: the washing machine by 1950 had become a wonderful synthetic creation of enameled steel, aluminum, Bakelite, and rubber. Gas and electric lighting were a revolution unto themselves. More and larger windows allowed light to penetrate homes, aiding housekeepers in their thorough removal of dust. However, this triumph over dust did not give women an opportunity to bathe in glory. Women became the guardians of an order that men, occupied with the affairs of street and work, cared little for or took for granted. Like dirt and dust itself, the art and labor of keeping a spick-and-span household were devalued by innovative cleaning machines and products and contested by a new generation of working daughters who had little time for and less interest in housework.[16] All this left the accomplished housewives of the first half of the century diminished in number and occupying a place as ambiguous in significance as the dust they cleaned. The housewife was swept to the edges of society, along with sanitarians, hygienists, and legions of others who once fought dust with the full accolades of an era that took itself to be locked in a life-and-death struggle against it.

INVISIBLE THINGS

Today, in industrialized societies, previous generations' great victory over dust is forgotten, especially by the young and well-off, even though ceaseless mopping-up operations must still be carried on throughout society. Dust and dirt, and all their ageless tiny allies, are less worrisome than such invisible fresh opponents as radioactivity and drug-resistant microbes. Our current neglect of dust shows in contemporary priests' failure to maintain the elaborate post-Communion ritual of cleaning up the crumbs of the Eucharist on the altar and in homeowners' propensity to use gasoline-powered blowers to shoot dust away from their own property with no concern for where it lands or what threat it might pose to public health. Because it no longer considers and fears dust as it once did, contemporary society (with many exceptions, especially when matters of personal hygiene and appearance are in play) no longer values cleaning and cleaners as highly.[17] The small of old is no longer as lethal as it was.

With order, sanitation, and cleanliness generally secured, society could begin to focus on the worst forms of pollution and contagion as defined by public sensibility and by emerging ranks of pathologists, pollution control officers, and epidemiologists. It is the profession of these forensic scientists of the environment to identify and remove microscopically toxic and contagious entities. No longer seen in itself as a threat, old-fashioned dust lost its place and its ability to command attention.

Ideas about dust have undergone a revolution in the last century and a half. Dust has been transformed from an enduring condition to an enemy of sanitary civilization, and then to a precise object of scientific knowledge and technological manipulation. At the same time, the discoveries of atoms and germs—and the whole network of microscopic entities and concepts they sustain—have redefined the minuscule and emphatically denied dust its role as humanity's primary gauge of smallness.

In this newly discovered microcosm, dust does not outsparkle its competitors in this magnificently intricate universe of little and particular things. Dust has been diminished and its real and metaphorical powers weakened.

With unprecedented control of water, light, and materials, industrial technology empowered society not only to remove dust but also to redefine it as distinct particulates. Dust lost its traditional associations with soil, dirt, and muck and became a multifaceted object of contemporary science. To use an analogy, dust, like its human counterpart the peasant, became in the city a more individualistic entity. In its most refined forms it lost all kinship with the dust of yesteryear and vanished into the microscopic suburbs of smallness.

In the city, dust became ever more particularized. In factories and laboratories it was analyzed, taken apart, and put together in entirely different ways. Dissected in light of new knowledge and technology, dust was no longer the clodhopper from the countryside. Instead it was caught up in science's discovery of the vastness and intricacy of the microcosm.

The contemporary history of dust straddles three paradoxes. First, the Industrial Revolution, which created so much dust and so many kinds of dust, also permitted society to regulate dust as never before. Second, at the same time that the great cleanup exposed dust to human sight and hand, specialists delineated entire undiscovered realms of entities smaller than dust. They did this with ever more precise instruments and tools. Just as people were being rescued from the tyrannies of dust, they found themselves introduced to legions of unseen things, things whose effect on personal and national well-being could not be denied. In sum, the majority found themselves having to make sense out of invisible lethal things whose existence they could not doubt but for whose observation and understanding they were not equipped.

Third, while science and technology have defined and ordered enormous microscopic realms, the elemental fear of the small persists. Indeed, it may have increased, fostered by growing expectations for a better life and armies of invisible things that threaten them. The unseen remains fraught with danger. Within its realm ancient bogeymen and ghosts are now joined by threats of extraterrestrials, cosmic rays, and stray meteorites. New discoveries induce new fears, which themselves can be compounded by fashionable obsessions and mass panic.

In the first half of this century, Western civilization was beset by the fear of germs. In the second half, this fear has been significantly supplanted by fears of radioactivity, environmental pollution, and, most recently, reinvigorated diseases. In differing forms, the old preoccupations with invisible enemies persist. However impressive science's conquest of the microcosm, the great majority has not fully accepted science's knowledge of and dominance over the small. Common prayers are still predicated on the premise that mind can control matter and that a merciful God—the God who numbers the hairs on our heads—will command individual cells and electrons to save human lives.

Surrendering human fate to the determined course of atoms does not befit a species that has not resigned itself to its return to dust. Indeed, this reluctance to be pulverized remains strong in those who have tasted the fruit of the pleasing garden of contemporary life. Our unwillingness to go gentle into that good night stems not just from a poet's exhortation but from membership in a civilization that, since the Middle Ages, has insisted on controlling things great and small—a civilization that has been less and less satisfied with leaving the details to the devil.

However, atoms and microbes—contemporary guides to the small and invisible—have forced people to confront realms of unseen entities and to consider the awesome power of small things. Though few people grasp these infinitesimal worlds, none can ignore their potency. Cells and computer chips, to mention two examples, illustrate the power of small things to captivate human thought and action. Dust itself, which once more than anything literally and metaphorically defined smallness and formed the gateway to the invisible, now is but a mere member of the expanding universe of the small. A century ago we hardly knew this universe existed.

CHAPTER ONE

OF TIMES WHEN DUST WAS THE COMPANION OF ALL

> In the sweat of thy face shalt thou eat bread, till thou return unto the ground; for out of it wast thou taken: for dust thou art, and unto dust shalt thou return. —Genesis 3:19

> If dust rises high and sharp, vehicles are coming; if it is low and wide, foot soldiers are coming. Scattered wisps of smoke indicate woodcutters. Relatively small amounts of dust coming and going indicate setting up camp. —Sun Tzu, *The Art of War*

In times before industry, when agriculture dominated, men and women were intimate with dust in ways beyond contemporary imagination. Dust accompanied them throughout their days. Although they saw many small and fine things, dust was commonly the smallest. For no one was this as true as for the peasant who lived by the earth.

After offering a definition and discussion of dust in the preindustrial world, this chapter looks at the relationship to dust of the European peasant of the Middle Ages. It does this not because European peasants were closer to or farther from dust than, for example, the first peasants of the agricultural revolution of ten thousand years ago in the Near East, or twentieth-century peasants of the remote countryside of Eastern Europe, Asia, or Africa. Rather, it dwells on medieval European peasants because they provide a gauge of Western civilization's ascent from fine and minute things for the few, to sanitation and cleanliness for the many, to our contemporary expert manipulation of the submicroscopic and atomic orders.

Throughout most of the world's history, dust was in the air, settling on the surfaces of things, piling up in dark corners of huts and castles. Even though most individual dust particles went unseen, dust as an entity functioned to mark the boundary of the small. Beyond that boundary an invisible and magical realm was believed to exist. Dust was formed, among other things, by the spores of mushrooms that exploded into the air, sprinkling their seed-bearing powder. It was formed by ultrafine airborne seeds (sometimes hundreds of thousands to a fraction of an ounce) or by "antbread," a barely visible part of a tiny seed that ants drag to their nests and which, if uneaten, springs up into plants.[1]

In its smallest and most deeply hidden forms, dust was too hermitic and magical to be understood. Yet its existence could not be denied. Its rising particles, shimmering in the light, appeared and disappeared before one's eyes. Finely ground dusts of plants and minerals put a telling taste in stews and made powerful medicines for the body, drugs for the mind, and even deadly poisons.[2]

Dusts brought smells: the unpleasant smells of the old, the stench of the pig farmer, the putrid breath from rotting teeth, and the pleasing scent of the fresh skin of one's lover. Unseen dusts circulated through the air, mingling with water vapor and forming snowflakes. Fire filled the air with the smell of burning wood, and the smell of sea salt could reach far inland when the winds were right.

There was no escaping dust in dry seasons, at harvest times, during great fires, or when volcanoes erupted. Dust accompanied the elements—fire, earth, air, and water—and it was like an element itself. Fire turned objects to ashes and soot, which are dusts. Water transformed earth to mud and dirt, which air dried and blew around as dust. Dust came from animals and plants, clung to bodies, and pervaded clothing. It filled dwellings whose walls, floors, and roofs were composed of mud and thatch. All over the world, people of times past fell asleep and woke up in dusty beds.

People made dust whatever they did. Human bodies themselves were dust mills. People made dust when they rubbed their hands together or ground food with their teeth (especially with their molars, whose etymological origin is *mola*, millstone). Out of human bodies came materials that over time would turn to dust: wax from the ears; mucus from the nose; phlegm, saliva, and vomit from the mouth; dandruff from the hair. From the anus came waste, which along with animal manure was plowed into the earth and made into soil. There it dried and became dust. The body itself was fodder for worms and provided manure for the earth. There was nothing on earth so big that it might not be made small.

However, dust was about more than discarded materials. Certain dusts not only provided essential goods but were treasured in themselves. Powdered spices flavored cooking. Specialized dusts served cosmetics and pharmacy with colors and powders to beautify, to soothe, to enchant, and to intoxicate. Animal and human wastes turn to powders, dusts that serve important purposes.[3]

Even in more recent times, at least among common folk, dust was taken to contain the essence of things. Common prescriptions forbade sweeping dust out the front door because it might take away a family's luck. "It must be swept inwards and carried out . . . then no harm will follow." Similarly, "if dust is swept out of the shop door, it is said to sweep away trade."[4] To clean a house or fireplace perfectly boded ill. Bodily wastes—associated with dust as a part of the earth— were understood to embody a person's essence and emanate special powers.[5] In medieval Europe, mummies from Persia were ground up and sold as medicine.[6] Folklore records the great healing powers of dust from the Communion table. After all, what could be more precious than the crumbs of the body of Christ? (Communion bread was made from the age's finest grain. It was marked triple-X in the Middle Ages and was not outranked until the end of the nineteenth century, when Pillsbury put four Xs on its bags of flour to suggest the ultimate in fineness.)[7]

DUST AS METAPHOR

In the metaphorical universe of opposites from which humans construct their cultural significance, dust and dirt form a negative pole. These half-brothers reside with the weak, the lowly, and the amoral.[8] Dust gathers with the rejected; found under beds, it was given the slang names beggar's velvet, house moss, and slut's wool. Dust is associated with death ("to bite the dust"), with insult ("eat my dust"), and with dismissal ("to dust off "). Dirt refers to what is morally compromising ("get the dirt on" or "throw dirt at" someone). A "speck of dust" or a "piece of dirt" are insignificant. In American slang, people of lower socioeconomic classes are described as "muck worms" or "mud sills." Lesser individuals are described as "chicken feed" and "crumb." To be a nobody is to be "a little snot" or "a little shit"; to be an ill-bred person is to be a "dreg" or a "grub."

Like its close associate, dirt, dust defined human experience from its beginning. Dust, in the form of soot and ashes, revealed where fire had burned and things had been transformed. Rising dust indicated commotion (hence the phrase "to kick up dust"). As any good ancient general or medieval *condottierre* knew, different forms of dust in the sky could indicate either distant enemy campfires or approaching armies.

Dust could mark human or climatic damage to the earth: wind erodes most severely where soils are finest and where they have been most abused. Blowing dusts could mark a barren land, like the Sahara Desert, or an abandoned city, like Tell Asma, northeast of Baghdad. They could be the source of the pall that hung over cities and poisoned lands and waters.[9]

Conversely, some dusts, such as gold dust, were regarded as the essence of the most valuable things. The finest dusts were considered to be the lightest earthly thing. In fairy tales, a mere sprinkle of dust could cause wondrous things to occur.

Dust's ambiguous metaphorical place as both the most ordinary and the finest of things derived from its role as a frontier between the seen and unseen. Like skin, a tissue that stands between the interior and the exterior, dust separated what could be known by the senses and what lay beyond them. In this respect dust was like darkness: it formed a graduated and permeable screen between the realm of what was empirically known and the realm of the imagined. In it images appear and vanish, things are transformed and even generated. Dust formed a shadowy realm that harbored secret exchanges and sponsored unexpected transformations. Associated with caves and cellars and other such places where neither light nor darkness entirely prevailed, dust was an ambiguous reservoir of important and unimportant, living and dead.

Human observation confirmed dust's elemental role in reality. All things broke down into smaller things. All matter could be made dust by force, fire, or rot. Dust—variegated and omnipresent—formed the elemental particles of everything on earth, except in the minds of a handful of classical atomists, who insisted that beyond dust there were yet smaller particles (atoms) that accounted for the making and unmaking of things.

People observed with their senses that the smallest living creatures—bugs, spiders, and worms—were creatures of dust. They generated spontaneously in dusty places. Worms appeared in compost piles, maggots formed in rotting meat, cockroaches were born from scraps of food that fell to the floor, and mice sprang out of dirty boxes left in undisturbed darkness.

People of the preindustrial, rural order grasped intuitively what contemporary people strain to imagine: the eternal cycle of all living things.

It made sense to them that God used spit and earth to make humans—after all, what else was available?—and they had no doubt that they, along with the mightiest monarchs, made good food for worms. People of earlier eras did not have to reach to comprehend Shakespeare's words, "A man may fish with the worm that hath eat of a king, and eat of the fish that hath fed of that worm."[10]

THE IMMORTAL STRUGGLE

Men and women of preindustrial times used the full possibilities of their culture to differentiate themselves from the small and degrading things to which the life cycle chained them. For the sake of continuity of self and the autonomy of being—for the angel within them—they strove to rise above the muck and slime, the worms and vermin, the gnats and ants that surrounded them.[11] With taboos and rituals against the contaminated and the polluted, and with elevating and sublimating religious conceptions, they sought to transcend the biology that ruled their bodies. They insisted that they were not just the dust grovelers, dirt eaters, and excrement makers they knew themselves to be. They would not have themselves reduced solely to the church's Lenten warning: "Memento, homo, quia pulvis es, et in pulverem reverteris." (Remember, man, of dust you are, and to dust you will return.)

In *Purity and Danger*, Mary Douglas offers another reason why people flee dust. She contends that dust and dirt are the detritus of cultural constructions of order.[12] Dust and dirt—leftovers, what the cookie cutter didn't cut—constitute a kind of disorder, an inchoate state of being, and thus a type of moral defilement. For twentieth-century people to understand this, Douglas counsels, they must set

Ant

aside current notions about taboos serving primitive hygiene codes and make an effort to conceive of dirt avoidance before it was shaped by modern bacteriology.[13] By freeing dust and dirt from recent concepts of pathogens and hygiene, contemporary people discover that dust and dirt were traditionally associated with transgressors and transgressions. To be dirty, or grovel in the dirt, connoted indecency and immorality.[14] Steering clear of dust and dirt sustained the cultural order, affirmed moral rectitude, and, most important, assured those who were clean that they were also morally pure.

Perhaps there is another reason why traditional people distanced themselves from dust and dirt. These substances are commonly associated with degeneration, which produces not just threats to bodily integrity but also the most unpleasant sensual experiences. The smell of putrefaction can cause people to vomit as a matter of physical reflex.[15] And with it comes the revolting sight of the oozing forms that accompany decomposition of organic materials. Its odd colors—dark reds, deep purples, and thick yellows—awaken fears of death. The white, almost translucent, maggots that accompany decomposition further evoke the threshold of chaos. The powers of the putrid, which contaminate dust by association, are concentrated in garbage piles, in compost heaps, and on battlefields. Every hunter, peasant, and cook knows that rot does death's work. It is no surprise that religious legends held that only the bodies of saints and devils escaped putrefaction after death.

DUST AND DIRT

Nineteenth-century Romantics, preferring the earthy people to the middle class, equated dirt with all things basic. Dirt—as soil, earth, and even manure—was for them the land's substance and the nation's moral nutrient. Dust, by contrast, was seen as removed from life. It belonged to the refined and the desiccated. In making this distinction the Romantics identified dirt as grit and ordure and dust as part of a cloud of vapor or smoke. This lineage is supported etymologically: The word *dirt* was borrowed from Old Norse *drit,* which goes back to a prehistoric German-based *drit* that also produced the Dutch *dreet,* or excrement.[16] Accordingly, in the thirteenth century dirt kept its primary association with smelly and unclean matter. Only in the seventeenth century—after the word *manure* (itself originally identical to *maneuver*) took on the meaning of dung that is spread and worked into the field— did *dirt* take on the meaning of mud and soil.[17]

Lighter than dirt, and more susceptible to winds and breezes, dust has often been associated with motion and commotion. It has even been made to stand for industry and progress, whereas dirt frequently is taken to belong to the land and thus to evoke the essence of a place. For this reason, dirt can be transformed into grounds for nostalgia. It can be made to evoke the soil, its touch and smell, and by extension the people who invested themselves in a given plot of earth. Dirt, in this metaphorical succession, also represents the old ways: hence the expression "a stick-in-the-mud."

As dirt can be emotionally expanded in meaning to represent life, so dust can be contracted in its meaning to connote only what is dry and desiccated, divested of animation, antithetical to life. It can be associated with the dead leaves blown by the wind or the emptiness and sterility of the wind itself. This contrast between dust's sterility and dirt's fertility has served literature in the past two centuries by characterizing types of people. There are dry-as-dust scholars—anemic, weightless representatives of a bookish sort of mind—and there are dirty men and women, a vital breed of humans who live on the land and, in sharp contrast to "the calculating bourgeoisie," are authentic in spirit and action. Romantics since Rousseau have prescribed a return to the countryside, to the land, to the very earth itself, as a spiritual cure for their disaffection. In *Crime and Punishment*, Dostoyevsky has Raskolnikov, the intellectual and murderer, kiss the ground at the crossroads to start on the true path to forgiveness.

As much as dust and dirt might be differentiated, they still shared earth as their mother. Both were dark and inferior. Both were identified with decay and death. Both belonged to the realm of the insignificantly small. The residue of discarded life, dust and dirt were trod underfoot and swept out, except by the most superstitious. Even Christ instructed his disciples to shake from their sandals the dust from a house in which they were poorly treated. And yet Christ mixed dirt with saliva to heal the blind.

Probably since the beginning of agriculture—whose origins lay in the Near East eight thousand years before Christ—court and city dwellers have labeled peasants as coarse, stinky, and worse.[18] If Snow White's wicked witch had asked of all history who was the *dirtiest* of them all, her mirror would undoubtedly have answered, "The peasant." No one was on more intimate terms with dust and dirt. Peasants were universally identified with the color of the earth they worked, as inferior, dark-skinned people. At the root of their inferiority was their proximity to dust and dirt.

Medieval European peasants lived mired in muck.[19] Even the medieval city, according to Lucien Febvre, wallowed in mud:

> The sunken road leading to the gate was muddy. Past the gate the street widened as it followed a capricious route through the town. A filthy stream ran down its center, fed by rivulets of liquid manure seeping from nearby manure heaps. It was a muddy slough in the rain, a desert of choking dust in the heat of the sun, in which urchins, ducks, chickens, and dogs, even pigs in spite of repeated edicts to control them, all wallowed together.[20]

Dust ruled peasants' homes as well. The kitchen, the most important room in the house because it contained fire and food, filled households with dust, soot, and smoke.[21] Historian Jerome Blum offers this portrait of the dwellings that housed the great majority of Europe's peasants from the early Middle Ages to the mid-nineteenth century:

> Most peasants lived in huts that were small, low, uncomfortable, and unhealthy. Many had only one room, or one room used as living

quarters and a second room that served for storage or as a stable. Not infrequently the floor was dirt. The hut held a few pieces of crude furniture that included a table, benches along the wall, a shelf or two and perhaps a cupboard, and, especially in eastern Europe, a large stove that took up much space in the crowded room. . . . Frequently there was no chimney, and the walls were blackened by smoke that could escape only through a hole poked in the roof wall. The small windows let in little light, so the hut's interior was dark, damp and gloomy.[22]

The poorest peasants were even worse off, living in filthy hovels and caves. Their beds were rubbish heaps. They were married to the rags they wore, the dirt that covered their bodies, and the smells of their bodily wastes.

As the Italian historian Piero Camporesi explains, peasants were infested by vermin and enveloped by disease.

[They were] dirty, almost always barefooted, legs ulcerated, varicose and scarred, badly protected by meager and monotonous diets, living in humid and badly ventilated hovels, in continuous, promiscuous contact with pigs and goats, obstinate in their beliefs, with dung heaps beneath their windows, their clothes coarse, inadequate and rarely washed, parasites spread everywhere—on their skin, in their hair and in their beds—their crockery scarce or nonexistent, often attacked by boils, herpes, eczema, scabies, pustules, food poisoning from the flesh of diseased animals, malignant fevers, pneumonia, epidemic flues, malarial fevers . . . lethal diarrhea (not to mention the great epidemics, the diseases of vitamin deficiency like scurvy and pellagra, the convulsive fits, so frequent in the past, epilepsy, suicidal manias and endemic cretinism).[23]

Peasants did not doubt that they were members of the biological kingdom.[24] Mites, lice, ticks, fleas, and mosquitoes—each had their sting and bite, and all made human beings their food and spawning grounds. A southern Italian peasant of the twentieth century declared the peasant's community with small and hurting things when he said, "We peasants are poor earthworms; we live with the animals, eat with them, talk to them, and smell like them. Therefore, we are a great deal like them."[25]

Human skin was vulnerable to dust and the creatures it nurtured. Historian Emmanuel LeRoy Ladurie said that sixteenth-century skin diseases were rife among peasants. They included "the itch, ringworm, scabies, leprosy, St. Anthony's Fire and St. Martial's Fire." Even peasant insults and curses made reference to "scrofula, fistulas of the thigh, ulcers and abscesses." "Villagers carried around with them a whole fauna of fleas and lice. Not only did they scratch themselves, but friends and relations from all levels in the social scale deloused one another. (The mistress deloused her lover, the servant her master, the daughter her mother.)"[26] The thumb was called the louse-killer *(tue-poux)*.

Although their macrocosm reached to the stars, peasants' lives and hopes revolved around small things. Not unlike contemporary people, they held on to scraps and remains to preserve the essence of belongings and loved ones. Medieval people often preserved fingernail clippings and locks of hair from the head of a deceased family patriarch in hopes of preserving the *domus*'s good fortune.[27]

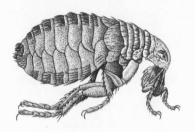

The human flea,
after Robert Hooke

The balance of the peasant world teetered on tiny grains. Peasants literally measured life by it. Grain meant food for today and seed for tomorrow. In good times, French peasants would respond to an inquiry about how they fared by saying, "J'ai du pain" (I've got bread). In bad times, they looked in the dust for things to eat. They dug up roots and ate rats and insects. Nothing was too small to be considered as food. According to the sixth-century bishop and historian Gregory of Tours, during famines people tried "to make bread out of virtually anything: grape pips, hazel tree flowers and even fern roots, and [their] stomachs were grossly distended because they had to eat field grass."[28]

During famines, which stalked European peasants until the nineteenth century, the smallest things could sway lives and fortunes. Peasants who lost their place on the land became wanderers. They scavenged the countryside for food, sought refuge in the woods, and flocked to the cities, where they lived under bridges, in piles of straw, or even in manure heaps. Beggars in tattered rags were everywhere—at the door, outside churches, in the marketplace—and they died like the flies that covered their decaying bodies.[29] Hunger real, hunger remembered, and hunger feared drove peasants from youth to the grave and kept them mired in dust well into the eighteenth century, making life for the majority, as Camporesi comments, "the antechamber of death."[30]

MIRED IN MUCK: ROYALTY AND ARISTOCRACY

Peasants were not the only medieval folk who were dirty and whose everyday encounters with the small made them itch and scratch. Kings and queens were also on intimate terms with vermin. Eugen Weber describes a young French princess in 1700 who had to be instructed "not to take lice, fleas, and other vermin by the neck to kill them in front of other people." The ladies of the French and Spanish courts were so familiar with vermin and perhaps just so bored with them that they "affected to train and feed pet fleas." In an age when running water was scarce and baths rare, kings and queens stank. Some were notorious: "The smell of Henry IV was so ferocious that his wife had to brew special perfumes to stand him, and Louis XIII [Henry's son] prided himself on taking after his father."[31]

Royalty commonly sucked aniseed lozenges to sweeten their breath, made foul by rotting teeth and bad digestion. With noses guarded by perfumed handkerchiefs, they picked their way through manure-filled streets. But neither riding horseback nor a haughty attitude could protect them from splashing mud, rising vapors, or swarming gnats. Diane Ackerman points out that Louis XIV kept a stable of servants to perfume his rooms with rose-water and marjoram and to wash his clothes in spices. "He insisted," she writes, "that a new perfume be invented every day." At his "perfumed court," "servants used to drench doves in different scents and release them at dinner parties to weave a tapestry of aromas as they flew around the guests."[32] Nevertheless, these birds could not mask the palace's stench for long, as the building's many small apartments were without running water.

While some royal personages were celebrity stinkers, royalty and nobility alike attempted to separate themselves from the rest of pungent humanity by adopting manners. Manners, according to Nobert Elias, were a way for high society to distinguish itself from dust and dirt.[33] In *Civility*, Erasmus taught the upper classes manners to distance themselves from the most incriminating of dirts, their own bodily discharges.

> To wipe the nose on the cap or sleeve belongs to rustics; to wipe the nose on the arm or elbow to pastry cooks; and to wipe the nose with the hand, if by chance at the same instant you hold it to your gown, is not much more civil. But to receive the excreta of the nose with a handkerchief turning slightly away from noble people is an honest thing.[34]

The high and mighty had to be taught how to react to the lowly stuff that came out of and resided on them. They had to learn not to disdain the picayune but to bring it—with the help of wig, makeup, razor, and toothbrush—under the control of civilized manners. After all, civilization was largely about appearance, and appearance required constant surveillance of the small stuff of the body. A single anecdote may reveal how far the manners of Europe traveled. In *A Canoe Voyage up the Minaysotor*, the English traveler George Fatherstonaugh described a U.S. federal judge he met in Wisconsin Territory in 1835:

The Court [title for the judge] and myself got along very well together. He had been bred to the law in the western country, did not
want for shrewdness, was good natured, but was evidently a man of
low habits and manners. He was very much amused with my apparatus for dressing, which was simple enough; a nail-brush was quite
new to him and he remarked that "it was a considerable better invention than a fork, which he said he had seen people use when they *had
too much dirt* in their nails." He "didn't see why I wanted so many
toothbrushes." He "once carried one, but it was troublesome, though
the handle was convenient to stir brandy-sling with."[35]

Travel in Europe in the eighteenth century offered similar experiences,
according to an English traveler, Arthur Young. Journeying through
France and Italy in 1790, he denounced a northern Italian inn: "Fright-
ful, black, filthy, and stinking, and there are no window panes." Things
improved for him in Turin and Milan but deteriorated again when he
boarded a decked boat from Venice to Bologna with a skipper who
"takes snuff, wipes his nose with his fingers, [and] cleans his knife with
his handkerchief at the same time he is preparing food for you."[36]

URBAN FILTH AND DISEASE

Besides lacking goods and means, European civilization until the twentieth century lacked a sufficient number of toothbrush-carrying Fa-
therstonaughs to clean up society. Even city dwellers' lives were clean
only by comparison to the dingy lives of peasants. Overcrowding filled
the cities and their dwellings to bursting point. Destitution, disease,
and vermin abounded. Without running water, sewage systems, paved

roads, or street lighting, even the best of cities were by today's standards rustic and foul. In London in the 1830s, the exiled and impoverished Italian social thinker Giuseppe Mazzini, unable to afford a cab, revealed his poverty by arriving at his appointments covered in mud. "The dirt in London streets appalled him. So did the bedbugs, which increased his nostalgia for Switzerland."[37] "Improper drainage," wrote Eugen Weber of European urban life, "was a great source of infection. Sewers and cesspits seeped into wells and cisterns." Some cities had oceans and rivers in which to dump sewage and garbage, but most "wallowed in wastes, . . . the excrement of daily life lapping round the feet of their citizens."[38] Of seventeenth-century London, Gamni Salgado observes, "Apart from Cheapside and Strand, London had no real streets to speak of, only narrow tracks that in wet weather stank with the slime of generations of filth and garbage, daily renewed by the discharge from doors and windows. Only when the plague ravaged the city was anything done about the piles of refuse that stood outside of every front door."[39]

Until the middle of the eighteenth century, European society was ensconced in darkness and mired in muck. The dainty and delicate were the exception. Dust, dirt, and muck multiplied and diminished according to the seasons, seemingly more at home with human beings than human beings were at home with them.

The worm literally and metaphorically connected men and women to the earth. They could not understand their relationship to the earth without reference to the work of the worm. Camporesi noted that men and women of the preindustrial age "lived—metaphorically and concretely—in a verminous universe, unimaginable today."[40] Popular ob-

Earthworm

sessions with worms at times swelled into contagions of fear. Within the imagined wilderness of the body, worms were savage beasts.

Not immune to this fear, physicians invented an invisible microcosm that explained illness as the behavior of unseen worms within the body. They postulated harmless worms, "innocent guests," which could become infuriated, bump up against the intestinal walls, and cause death. They claimed that sick worms defecated within the human body and their excrement befouled human blood, causing cardialgia, hiccups, stomach pains, headaches, convulsions, and epilepsy.[41]

Worms, which along with snakes crawled in and out of skulls in medieval mortuary art, penetrated both the popular consciousness and medical debates.[42] They evoked the horror of being consumed and digested in the darkness of the coffin. Besides stimulating confessions and intensifying wishes for a heaven, worms served the era's science. In *The Cheese and the Worms*, Carlo Ginzburg explains how worms figured in the cosmos of a sixteenth-century miller who was burned at the stake by the Roman Inquisition for heretical ideas. The miller, Menocchio (whose name means "little eye"), drew an objectionable analogy: "From the most perfect substance of the world [the angels] were produced by nature, just as worms are produced from a cheese, and when they emerged received will, intellect, and memory from God as he blessed them." The miller argued that God himself was spontaneously generated out of chaos, the first "great and crude matter."[43] In Menocchio's view, heaven itself was consumed by the subterrestrial microcosm of worms.

Menocchio was not alone in conjuring up dark images of invisible enemies, even though a certain degree of orthodoxy could be maintained by contending that not even worms inside the body could escape the all-seeing eye of God or the devil's machinations. The evil that had led the world astray was explained by invisible demons who festered in feces. These demons transformed themselves into legions of worms, flies, spiders, and bats. In the form of scourges and clouds of locusts, they attacked human fields. It was the devil's cunning, people said, that taught rats to flee houses falling to ruin and worms to escape the body of a dying person. "A quite certain sign and portent of [death] was the flight from dying flesh of these slimy and very sticky inhabitants of the dark, warm and damp recesses of the body."[44] The small and the invisible always required explanation and proved to be an open medium for human imagination.

The human beings of the preindustrial world could not escape, and therefore could not think beyond, the boundaries of dust, darkness, and skin. To transcend these limitations would require a great cleanup of the human environment. Water and light would have to be turned against earth and darkness. Clean, shiny goods would have to be created in vast quantities. Knowledge of the small and the invisible would have to become the concern of a new breed of curious men and women with new theories and machines. But first a fresh and acute view of the microcosm, along with a brand new order of fine goods and instruments, would have to be created. In the late Middle Ages and Renaissance, curious scientists and thinkers breached the frontiers of dust, darkness, and skin as no other civilization in the West ever had.

CHAPTER TWO

OLD METAPHORS AND NEW MEASURES OF THE MICROCOSM

Col tuo lume me levasti.
(With your light you raised me up.)
—Dante, *Paradiso* 1.74–75

As ideas of refinement and, later, cleanliness took hold of European courts and the emerging urban business classes in modern and early modern history, peasants were correspondingly considered dirty and coarse. Indisputably, they were the closest companions of dust. They lacked the manners of the residents of city and court, and they sorely lacked delicate things. Though nature occasionally presented these people of the earth with beautiful objects—a spider's web, the etchings of frost on a leaf—none of the things they owned were refined.

What was small in everyday peasant life started with the self and proceeded downward: from cat and rat to spider, ant, and flea. The small was what could be taken in one's hands—what could be gleaned from a field, lifted up in the air, rolled between one's fingers, and put in one's mouth. The extremely tiny encompassed all the things that could barely be seen: things that glimmered in and out of sight or flickered like ash in a cooling fire.

Peasant's dwellings were dark and dusty. Their breads were coarse. Centuries away from finely granulated sugars, their sweetener was honey, which varied enormously in flavor and quality from one locale to another.[1] Their homes were devoid of furniture, windows, or closets and were unadorned with fancy cloth or woodwork. Peasants rarely sat in chairs and never read books; they might never even see a picture. They never looked at themselves in a mirror or peered through a glass window. They rarely, if ever, handled coins, and they knew nothing of precious gems.

They were, however, dazzled by gold, the antithesis of dirty dust. Gold cured diseases, especially of the eye. Under gold's luminous and spellbinding power, peasants, as medieval historians remarked, were occasionally caught up in digging crazes. No magic was greater than that which could turn common earth into precious gold. No adventure was as worthy as Columbus's search for a shortcut to the Orient and its gold and spices.

Peasant tools were as simple and coarse as their lives. They lacked the knowledge—and even the wish—to shape fine belongings. If they had musical instruments, they too were simple—often a mere reed whistle or a hide drum to beat on. They lacked the instruments necessary to create fine things. They were without glasses to see or pencils to record minute objects. They lived in a world without miniatures, and they shared one of the most common prejudices of the old order: What is small is, with rare exceptions, insignificant, despicable, and common as dust.

In this rural world, small things went unmeasured. Peasants lacked fine rulers and scales, and they had no need for precise measurement or calculation. They had no gauges to record pressure, no meters to measure power, no detectors for smoke or gases, and no thermometers. They had no means for calculating volume or speed or ascertaining conversions between liquids, solids, and gases. Belonging to a rude and coarse world, overshadowed by dust and darkness, they had neither desire nor knowledge to manipulate minute things. The scale of the small remained, as it had been seemingly forever, the sparrow in the field and the hairs on one's head. No one spoke then of etching on a computer chip a hundred times finer than a human hair.

SCALES OF MEASURE

Besides having no need to calculate precisely, medieval peoples lacked standardized measures to do so. Measurements varied immensely from one locale to another. Business proceeded by estimates. Distances were judged by how far a team of oxen could plow between rests, by how far a man could walk in a day, or, in Old French Canada, which more than anywhere else in North America preserved the old regime, by the number of bowls of tobacco a man could smoke on his way to his destination. Lengths were determined by the average size of a human thumb, hair, or forearm, while quantities were subject to such widely varying measures as baskets, barrels, casks, and cartloads.[2] The few common standards were established by local authorities. As every traveling merchant knew, measures varied greatly between regions.

The most precise measures were used for the most precious things. These units were derived from the finest common thing of the era: a kernel of grain. Grain was a traditional denomination of Sicilian currency. Edward II of England, in an effort at modernization, defined an inch, formerly the thickness of a man's thumb, to be "equal to three grains of barley, dry and round, placed end to end lengthwise."[3] Long before the Middle Ages, peoples of the Middle East measured the weight of diamonds by carob beans *(qirat)*; hence the carat became the unit of weight for precious stones.

Things did not change in the countryside (especially the countryside remote from trade routes) until kings and their representatives took hold of them. Then rulers insisted on defining rules. The French Revolution brought the metric system to France and to the rest of continental Europe, setting in place for all a standardized mathematical grid for exploring, quantifying, systematizing and controlling the small in everyday life. Universal standards marked the triumph of a new society in which goods would be more equally and carefully partitioned.

The farther cities progressed in wealth and specialization, the more precise they became and the farther they left peasant villages behind. Even in cities, however, the rate of progress was comparatively slow as long as their populations were tethered to agriculture. Great machines and delicate instruments remained scarce until the Industrial Revolution.

FIRST EXPLANATIONS OF THE MICROCOSM

The medieval understanding of the microcosm—all those things smaller than the human being—derived from a mixture of experience and tradition. The first premises about the small were drawn from Greek and Christian views of the macrocosm, the heavens, where the sun, planets, and stars made manifest the glory of God.[4] The church, the dominant authority of intellectual life, had little interest in what philosophers might speculate about the little things of earth, as long as God was not denied as creator, Christ as savior, and man as worthy of salvation.[5]

In scholastic thought—the fusion of philosophy and theology that characterized the highest reaches of medieval thought—the four earthly elements were fire, gas, water, and earth. The planets, stars, and invisible orbs were composed of a fifth element called celestial ether, whose heavenly characteristics made it the subtlest material in the universe. The new science of physics that developed in the Middle Ages agreed with this view. (Even early twentieth-century physics postulated ether as a hypothetical means for the transmission of light and heat.) Less corruptible and immutable than the other elements and more transparent to God's light, celestial ether had causative influences on earth.[6] Living things were argued to be superior to inanimate material because they contained the spark of life ("a fly, a flea, and a plant are absolutely nobler than the heavens"). Nevertheless, this belief did not deny heaven's influence over the earth and all its creatures. There was a general adherence to the Aristotelian notion that celestial bodies played a role in the generation of living things, and a corresponding adoption of a second notion that there were two kinds of living things: those "born by means of seeds," which scholastics called "perfect animals," and those "spontaneously generated from decaying matter, as were a number of insects, from within by secretions from the organs of animals." Thomas Aquinas argued that, while the perfect animals require a seed (*virtus particularis*), the imperfect animal, testifying to heavenly light's power over dust and darkness, is generated by the sun's universal power (*universalis virtus*) and is a direct consequence of the putrefaction the sun induces.[7]

Satisfied with explaining lowly earth by means of the mighty heavens—the inferior microcosm by the superior macrocosm—scholastic thinkers left the minuscule largely unobserved and unexplained. Such earthly phenomena as how plants grow and reproduce did not have a role in philosophers' ethereal concerns; they were the province of folklore and mythology. There were exceptions, like Adelard of Bath, a scholastic who argued that, though plants spring from dust by God's will, humans are not justified in simply pronouncing their growth a miracle and seeking no further understanding. Adelard contended that nature had a system, and that only when human knowledge "fails miserably should there be recourse to God."[8]

The medieval thinker's proclivity to treat all subjects rationally and the importance of this in the formation of science should not be underestimated; nor should we underestimate reason's role in the examination of the microcosm. The first scholastic explanations of the universe that took into account natural causes arose in the early twelfth century at the school of Chartres. Inspired by Plato's book on creation, the *Timaeus*, the members of this school depicted the world as composed of interactive particles of the four elements: earth, water, air, and fire. Lacking the sophistication of Democritus, the Greek atomist of the fifth century B.C. who conceived of the action of indivisible atoms governing the mutation of all visible things, they nevertheless believed the elements to be mutually transformable. In their conception, the elements were arranged in concentric spheres with earth in the center, water next, then air, and finally fire, forming a finite spherical universe in which the elements tended to gather together in mass.[9]

This universe contained no void. Space was a plenum. Movement occurred by the small pushing on the small. Sensations resulted from the motion of particles in the body. Sight was explained as the eye emitting rays that were met by fire particles emitted by objects. Sound was the motion of air particles, without reference to the eardrum. Tastes and odors also came from emitted particles.

By the thirteenth century, speculators on the invisible realms of nature had access to a range of Greek, Latin, and Arab scientific texts.[10] The philosopher and naturalist Albertus Magnus (Thomas Aquinas's mentor) offered keen observations on animals and plants and speculated on the formation of rocks and mountains. Demonstrating an acutely empirical spirit, in the thirteenth century the Holy Roman Emperor Frederick II, of Sicily, made remarkable observations on birds and their anatomy, habitats, and behavior. Other thinkers, as if to peer into the elements, reflected on invisible processes such as sound, vacuums, and magnetism; others considered such natural phenomena as condensation, melting, and the spread of diseases. The last they attributed to vapors, an explanation that remained popular until the articulation of germ theory in the nineteenth century. A handful of thinkers conjectured the origins of human sperm, suggesting its source to be excess food and its origin to be any part of the body. They distinguished two types of blood, arterial and venous. They pointed to the heart as the seat of the soul and the first source of bodily heat, another invisible phenomenon they found worthy of reflection.

However, it was in optics and meteorology, at that time a single subject, that thirteenth century thought shone.[11] Between earth and moon, the changing worlds of fire and air were on display. Above there were shooting stars and comets, the rays of the sun, and the comings and goings of the weather. The appearances and causes of rain, snow, droughts, and storms all merited explanation. Medieval thinkers questioned rainbows, false suns, and light passing through air and water. They considered such subtle realities as transparency, refraction, illumination, and magnification. Subjects that demanded both observation and geometry offered the privilege of working with light, the most ethereal part of God's creation.

Admittedly, by twentieth-century measures, medieval natural science neglected the minute. Medieval thinkers constructed meaning out of metaphor and analogy rather than by observation and enumeration. With their capacity for reason they posited the existence of great and mighty things on high; yet with their faith they knelt before the baby Jesus lying in humble hay. They pondered such intangible matters as theology, morality, and humanity's journey toward God.[12] Exploration into the precise details of natural phenomena was blocked by a preference, which classical physics would sustain, for celestial matters and by an adherence to an Aristotelian teleology that defined things by their place in the cosmos rather than by observing their actual functions.[13]

MUCH REMAINS HIDDEN

Little in their world pointed medieval minds or imaginations toward the microcosm. Medieval technology and industry did not demand mastery of the small. The most curious scientists lacked instruments and institutions to focus their visions on the particular. Ignorance of atomic and molecular theory kept the most advanced thinkers in the dark about a vast range of natural phenomena.

Without a theory of atoms as the basic unit of reality, as the building blocks of all matter—something that science did not regain until the end of the sixteenth century with the revival of the classical atomism of Democritus and Lucretius—much of the microcosm could be neither conceived nor articulated.[14] Without microscopes, which scientists began to utilize in the sixteenth and seventeenth centuries, much that was minuscule simply went unobserved. Myriad realms and processes remained concealed—covered by dust, obscured by darkness, buried below earth and skin. Even when bits and pieces of the microcosm were glimpsed, they were explained in reference to the existing cosmology and folklore. Nevertheless, medieval and Renaissance thinkers did affirm a fundamental element of all scientific inquiry: they proclaimed the preeminence of reason and used it to explore and explain the world, thus laying the conceptual foundation for modern science.[15]

In the Renaissance, the philosophy of naturalism combined science with poetry and used metaphor and allegory to describe nature's hidden meaning. As Robert Lenoble suggests, nature became a set of signs and ciphers to be divined by magic and the science of signatures.[16] Astrology was taken seriously. The heavens augured the future; fate and providence expressed themselves by means of shooting stars. Nymphs peopled fountains and rivers, and the sea was thought to clean itself in the light of a full moon. Trees were taken to have the same "blood" that circulated in animals. The world was considered conscious and living, "like a vast animal, warm and tempered by the heavens."[17]

Below the earth, in the veins of gems, flowed a life spirit that nursed stones and allowed them to multiply. Individual stones were classified by their proximity to precious metals and, by the sixteenth-century geologist John Kentman of Dresden, according to "marks on their surface or by their resemblance to the sun, moon, or stars, or things in nature such as fruit."[18]

Folk healers and herbalists also dabbled in and tinkered with the world of the small. They mixed plant and animal bits with dusts and oils and fused knowledge with superstitions. A few plied the secrets of alchemy, a twelfth-century Arab import into the West, seeking to change base materials into precious metals. With furnaces, laboratories, and charts of affinities, they pursued a belief system not without significance for the birth of modern science and not without similarities to the modern periodic table of the elements. They intended to weigh and number the smallest things and processes in nature.

Turning dust and dirt into silver and gold made alchemy seem to Renaissance experimenters a science worth its salt and spice.[19] Alchemy grew in popularity until science transformed it into charlatanry, until nineteenth-century chemistry—a new kind of "subterranean physics"—began to pick apart the earth, compound by compound, molecule by molecule, and found the reason and the means to transform the earth's smallest particles into useful things.[20] Alchemy's language of natural creation and its promise of ennobling metals were consigned to the dustbin of history, as it "gave way to public utility, [its] marvels and curiosities to facts, wonder to reason, and *fortuna* to human agency and state discipline."[21] Even if night could not be turned into day, darkness into light, or dust into gold, the new alchemy instructed on an immense scale what the oldest mining taught: money could be made taking apart the earth chunk by chunk and selling it bit by bit.

However, this knowledge lay in the distant future. Until recent times, only hermetic and magical processes were believed to bring precious metals out of the earth and to transform dust and dirt into things that please and cure. Magic seemed entirely reasonable in an age when delicate and fine things—the highest goods of civilization—were scarce for everyone, and when humans could only see indistinctly and measure roughly and were incapable of discovering and controlling the treasures of heaven and earth. Beyond mind, measure, and machine, the goods of the earth belonged to ordinary dust and dirt, and to all the invisible entities within and beyond them. Only a truly mighty chemistry would make the world over in the image of human knowledge and desires.

CHAPTER THREE

EARLY DISCERNMENT
OF THE MINUTE

> Because we see these [beautiful] things owing to our eyes the soul
> is content to stay imprisoned in the body; for through the eyes all
> various things of nature are represented to the soul.
> —Leonardo da Vinci, *Notebooks*

> I see nothing but infinities on all sides which surround me as an
> atom, and as a shadow which endures only for an instant and is no
> more. —Blaise Pascal, *Pensées*

A European peasant's eyes would have opened wide the first time he
entered a thriving medieval city. In its churches and palaces, he would
have seen ivory panels on imperial diptychs and the delicate designs
of illuminated gospels decorated with silver, gilt, enamel, and gems.
He would have been stunned by golden mosaics and the intricate carving, embossing, enameling, and inlaying that had begun to appear on
such treasured items as the crown of Conrad in 1027 and the bronze
doors of the great medieval churches of Germany and Italy.[1]

In the churches the peasant would have encountered colorful vest-
ments woven with shiny metal threads and intricately carved altars,
pulpits, and confessionals. He would have seen frescoes whose techniques were more precise, colors richer, lines subtler than anything he

had ever imagined. He would have been overwhelmed by both the representation and the miniaturization of life. In these works of art life was depicted as free of the dust and dirt that shaped the painful, granular contours of his own daily life.

In the cathedral—especially if it were a later Romanesque or, in Italy, one of the rare Gothic churches—he would have seen the great light shows. With enlarged windows of decorated glass, natural light (not the shadowy light of candle and torch) streamed in. Light embodied order and value. The antithesis of darkness, dirt, and dust, it was the purest extension of God's grace and his first creation. Light stood for God's invisible wisdom, warm mercy, and pure love.[2] Free of noise and squalor, the church suggested the illuminated beauty and order of an everlasting, but as yet invisible, kingdom. In every way the church stood in contrast to the earthy life the peasant knew and the dark, stinking pits of hell where resided "the worm that does not sleep."[3]

Dante's *Paradiso* shared the ideal that informed the churches, aspiring to the love and light of God's abode. Synonyms for light form a stairway to the celestial creator—*candore, facella, favilla, fiamma, fiore, folgore, fuoco, lucerna, lumera, raggio, scintilla, sole, splendore, stella.* Light, Beatrice instructs Dante, "is an expression of God's Being. Every light . . . has its origin in God," and the heavens and all things below partake of this light.[4] Dante travels upward from the world of strife and anger, the things that prick and bind earthly humans, believing he follows the light that ascends to the love that sustains all.

In guilds and artisans' shops, the peasant would have seen men at work on larger but still sublime objects. Coin engraving in the thirteenth century and the manufacture of dies in the fourteenth century reflected Western civilization's growing capacity to manipulate metals. Ironically, improvements in the making of swords and armor advanced simultaneously with the perfection of firearms and of the deadly dust gunpowder. Illustrating that even then civilization relied on control of little objects, medieval artisans learned to manufacture a range of tools such as needles, drill bits, and braces. If these tools did not give artisans control of a particulate like dust, they at least offered an ability to command little things.

The capacity to make intricate things went hand in hand with keener measuring. Anticipating twentieth-century science, medieval astronomers chose accuracy of measurement over theories of physics and metaphysics. Mariners and instrument makers concerned themselves with matters in which a single degree could make an enormous difference. They used empirical measures and achieved accuracies that made academic scientists seem long on words and circuitous in their ways. Metallurgists, attempting to produce alloys of consistent quality, learned to measure the density of metals. Assayers, seeking to value coins and jewelry, learned to weigh to a precision of about 0.1 milligram.[5] Fine things and fine measures were things a fine civilization could not have enough of.

As the civilization advanced in measuring and calibrating tangible things, it also moved forward in calculating so intangible a thing as time. Nothing testified as much to the era's skills with gears and levers as the mechanical clock. The large clock on the cathedral or the palace would surely have caught the peasant's interest with its seemingly automated movement, its bright colors, and its parade of figures that measured the passing hours. This accurate portrayer of untouchable time, with its intricately meshed gears, was also the queen of all the mills that, starting in the third quarter of the twelfth century, collectively drove Western civilization's commerce forward. Prominently placed on the face of the city's most important buildings, the clock evinced the age's impulse to quantify and command. Henri de Vick's mechanical clock, which divided the day into twenty-four equal hours, "was set up on the Palais Royal in Paris in 1370. King Charles V ordered all churches in Paris to ring the hours and quarters according to de Vick's clock."[6] Lewis Mumford judged the clock to be "the key engine of the modern industrial age . . . prophetically the accurate automatic machine."[7] It foreshadowed an age when great machines would dominate the small and make new kinds of dusts.

In the workshops of a large fifteenth-century Italian city, the peasant would have encountered artisans taming the small with carpentry, leatherwork, weaving, and cloth making (the latter supported by the new fourteenth-century flax crusher).[8] A commentator in 1462 numbered "beautiful Florence's" crafts:

> [It] has 66 spice shops and 84 workshops [that] belong to woodworkers, intarsia [wood, metal, and ivory inlaying] designers and wood carvers, and it has 54 workshops specializing in the carving of stone, both marble and sandstone; and there are masters with great skill in

carving and relief and in half relief and foliage work both outside and inside the city . . . and there are also 30 workshops for goldbeaters and workers in silver thread and there are inspired masters of wax images equal to others throughout the world . . . and there are 44 workshops of goldsmiths and silver workers and jewelers in the city.[9]

Certain crafts reached new levels of perfection in Renaissance Florence. One was metalwork, which was spectacularly on display in the great metal doors of Brunelleschi's Duomo and in Donatello's sculpture of David. Printing, which developed in the fifteenth century under Gutenberg and his followers, was another art of refinement and miniaturization. With the perfection of type design and the use of artificial scripts, printing responded to the increased demand for books by a growing literate laity. Books—which over the ages would so change Western civilization's experience of the world—were the richest human miniature. In their minuscule spaces, composed of rows of letters and thin pages, invisible worlds were imagined. Even though books produced their own distinct dust, they promised—as no other earthly thing had—to preserve writer and reader from death. Produced in unprecedented quantities and at the best prices in Venice and other Italian cities, books—great and miniature—were windows on unseen worlds. A book invited even the dirtiest reader into shimmering palaces to meet the fairest princesses.

If our peasant had visited Venice, he would have encountered a third craft that opened the door to the small: glassmaking. By the middle of the fifteenth century, Venice's most sophisticated glassmakers were making the first pure white glass, *cristallo,* an improvement over medieval colored or tinted glass.[10] Anticipating a bright and shiny world four centuries hence, glassmakers admitted and reflected light into a dark and dreary world. Better lighting allowed more small things to be seen. Venice successfully guarded its glassmaking secrets until the late seventeenth century, when the French produced the plate glass that would adorn the Hall of Mirrors at Versailles for Louis XIV, the "Sun King."

By the end of the fifteenth century, Venetian glassmakers were crafting mirrors, which seductively offered to let onlookers gaze on their own image and do what they would to improve it for the eyes of the world. "Along with the development of the large looking glass during the sixteenth and seventeenth centuries, hand mirrors and pocket mirrors reached the height of popularity. Pocket mirrors were an essential part of dress, as shown in portraits of the [mirror-holding] beauties of those days."[11] Mirrors—first for looking at oneself and later for decorating one's rooms—reflected a new concern with individuality. This new perspective was accompanied by a growing wish for a cleaner, brighter world—a world truly distant from dirty peasants, who saw their image reflected back to them only in pools.

Eyeglasses developed along with mirrors and books. Their lenses offered a means of perceiving tiny and distant things. Though their origin is uncertain (generally located somewhere near Pisa around 1300), it is clear that by the sixteenth century Europeans were putting on glasses to look closely at small things and to read. In 1582, Henry IV of France passed statutes to regulate the mirror- and glassmakers in cities, who were setting up prosperous shops while their poorer counterparts traveled by foot out to villages to hawk glasses, chanting a description of their wares:

> I have spectacles for the old,
> Monocles which do miracles,
> Glasses for snakes and peacocks.
> I have them for all usage.
> To put on the big noses of the wise,
> To correct the sight of fools,
> Render clairvoyant the jealous.[12]

ARTISTS PIERCE THE DARKNESS

If our peasant wanted to see the most delicate work of all, he would have done well to look into an artist's studio. By the end of the fifteenth century, the best artists were the observers and engineers of the age. They were light's most faithful servants, piercing the darkness, removing dust, and grasping essential but intangible forms. More than all other craftsmen, artists were expected to observe and render the world.[13] A product of urban Italian society, their achievement was a rational control of materials in their painting, sculpture, and music.[14] Experimentation accompanied their art. They considered such empirical matters as the qualities of paints, the precise characteristics of metals, and the details of chasing, embossing, gilding, and inlaying.

Artists' studios were the laboratories of the precise and delicate; painters' renderings stood unrivaled until the advent of photography in the nineteenth century. By the fifteenth century, artists were the keenest of human observers.[15] They perfected ways of looking at the world and representing it. They did all they could to let light enter their crowded shops and studios and fall on their canvases. Leonardo distinguished between lighting in the shop of the painter and that of the sculptor. He specifically mentioned the desirability of having light from the north when drawing from nature.[16]

Artists idealized nature as free of dust and dirt, showed the contours of the human body, and represented animals, plants, and cities. They sought a person's inner character in the mirror of the face—the glint of an eye, the curl of a lip. To depict nature accurately, they perfected the representation of volume, mastered perspective and foreshortening, extended their range of colors, and developed the use of tints and hues. These skills made them masters of the microcosm.

In their quest to compose beauty out of what the eye sees, they contradicted those who went before them. Earlier thinkers like Robert Grosseteste, who anticipated Descartes's and Newton's work on optics, had explored light as the first corporeal form of material things and the first principle of motion and efficient causation.[17] With their bold reach, Gothic architects staged light as the manifestation of God's wisdom, grace, and being. In contrast, Renaissance artists rendered light as seen in the world and the world as seen by light. Sixteenth-century Italian artists like Correggio, Titian, and Raphael displayed their mastery of light, painting their subjects in dark rooms lit by candles and fireplaces or gathered around campfires at night. They depicted the penumbra of darkness, the incandescence of fires, and the cool, faint glow of a coming dawn.[18]

Civilization depends on control of the small, which in turn requires mastery of light. The eye must see before the hand can draw. Objects must be brought out from behind dust and darkness before they can

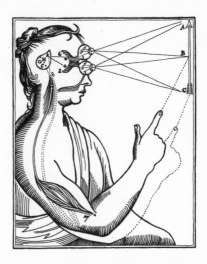

Descartes's theory of perception, 1677,
shows the nerve impulse traveling from
the eye to the pineal gland and on to
the muscles

be rendered beautiful. On this count, Renaissance artists took a great step into the world of small things. Indeed, the artist was Europe's first and keenest naturalist, a required member of every expedition. Drawing was an art that every scientist tried to master.[19] The artist assembled an interesting world of small things, detailing the neighborhood of dust and dirt.

THE MASTER EYE

In observation and illustration Leonardo da Vinci—artist, engineer, and inventor—was the master eye of master eyes.[20] It is fitting that he (a villager with only a few years of education) began his apprenticeship painting angels' wings. His creations, true heirs of Botticelli's slender, fair-skinned, golden-haired cherubs, were suffused with airiness and grace. No theme seemed too subtle for Leonardo to capture—not the intangibles of beauty, goodness, and vice, the movements of whirl-winds, the body of a descending bird, or the distortions of weight and aging on the human body.

As Leonardo constructed perfect lathes and designed machines to explore below the seas and fly into the skies, he also penetrated the screen of skin in order to understand the inner workings of animal and human bodies. Based on dissections of more than thirty human bodies, his anatomical drawings were so exact that they, along with those of Vesalius's classic of anatomy, *The Fabric of the Human Body* (1543), were still used in European medical schools hundreds of years later.[21] According to George Sarton, "Anatomical drawings of the soft internal parts of the body are extremely difficult, and some of them made by Leonardo more than 450 years ago have never been equaled. Photographs, however good, cannot always replace them."[22]

Leonardo advanced the sight of medieval science, which had already described plagues, dissected bodies, and performed surgery.[23] With the tools of neither anatomy nor physiology available and with medicine subservient to convention rather than open to observation, the inner world of living things persisted as a hidden realm—yet Leonardo insisted on exploring it.[24] He sought nature's inner secrets by investigation, dissection, and observation. His *Notebooks* are filled with exhortations to himself to examine and explain. In a section on anatomy, he wrote, "Make the rule and give the measurement of each muscle, and give the reasons of all their functions, and in which way they work and what makes them work &c." In a section entitled "Zoology and Comparative Anatomy," he wrote of "the flight of the 4th kind of butterflies that consume winged ants." Elsewhere he instructed himself to "procure the placenta of a calf " and "describe the tongue of the woodpecker and the jaw of a crocodile." In a section titled "Of the Eyes in Animals," he wrote, "The eyes of all animals have their pupils adapted to dilate and diminish of their accord in proportion to the greater or less light of the sun or other luminary [*sic*]. But in birds the variation is much greater; and particularly in nocturnal birds, such as horned owls."[25]

After Leonardo and the Renaissance, medicine, especially surgery, whose practitioners worked by necessity more empirically than doctors, increasingly proceeded on observation rather than precept—even if the precepts came from the mighty Hippocrates, Galen, or Avicenna. Throughout the sixteenth century and into the seventeenth, the learned humanists gave way, if grudgingly, to the detailed findings of the new anatomists, physiologists, and clinicians.[26] When the great screen of flesh was pierced, a few bold explorers entered a new territory of the small.

NEW INSTRUMENTS, NEW SCIENCE

The artist's monopoly over the minute was first challenged by a handful of scientists in the seventeenth century. With telescope and microscope, mathematics and experimentation, they discovered and sketched a new microcosm. Aided by newly invented instruments, scientists discovered and described realms that Leonardo could never have seen.

Even without the aid of a microscope, Paracelsus (1493?–1541) had articulated the kernel of a new medicine. Challenging Galen's humor theory of disease, he suggested that every disease had a precise origin and a particular remedy. This proved to be a decisive idea in the development of pharmacology, one of the emerging sciences of small things.[27] Later, still without a microscope, but by keen observation and incisive reasoning, William Harvey (1578–1657) opened a door to the microcosm. Like the global explorers of the seas, he explored an undiscovered country: the human body.[28] Harvey showed that the heart, and by extrapolation the rest of the body, functioned like a machine. Foreshadowing an understanding of cells as factories, he deduced the functioning of the circulatory system and declared the heart to be a great pump. Harvey wrote: "[The heart] deserves to be styled . . . the sun of our microcosm just as much as the sun deserves to be styled the heart of the world."[29]

In the first decade of the seventeenth century, Galileo scanned the heavens. His telescope added insult to injury when he pointed out that there were imperfections in the newly discovered and defiant heliocentric galaxy: Jupiter had moons, there were spots on the sun, and the Milky Way itself was a collection of distinct stars. Distant dots in the sky gave rise to arguments about the very design of creation. Galileo also pointed his telescope earthward and peered into an insect's eyes.

New instruments allowed seventeenth-century scientists to penetrate farther into the microcosm.[30] Scientists made radical use of a range of precise devices. In his classic book *On the Magnet* (1600), William Gilbert used a seaman's compass to create a science out of the medieval mysteries of lodestones and magnetism. The invention of the air pump, made possible by suction pumps that allowed miners to penetrate farther below the earth's skin, served science in the hands of Robert Boyle (1627–1691). He undertook experiments on the question of what happens to things deprived of air. He showed that life, combustion, and sound die without air, whereas light continues to shine through a vacuum. On the basis of additional work on the transformation of gases into liquids, Boyle advocated the "atomic explanation of matter: that small matter consists of small, hard, indestructible particles that behave with regularity."[31] The most imaginative students of science began to realize that the universe concealed a miniature order as perfect as that of the heavens.

Other measuring devices such as the thermometer, barometer, pendulum clock, and above all the microscope permitted new levels of precision.[32] The microscope, whose invention can be attributed to Zacharias Janssen, a Dutch spectacle maker, in 1590, or to Galileo, who announced his invention in 1610, opened the door to the realm of the truly small and invisible. In the seventeenth century, masters of the microscope passed beyond the boundary of dust into the suburbs of microscopic life. Under their lenses, legions of living things never before seen, dubbed animalcula, ate, reproduced, and died. The microscopists drew the external anatomy of insects, capturing antennae, eyes, and legs in detail. They completed the mapping of Harvey's circulatory system by actually observing the "minute and capillary channels" between the arteries and veins. And they showed that seedless plants, like the fern, were teeming with fertile dusts: "such is the wonderful and minutely fine dust inherent to the back of fronds of ferns."[33]

Marcello Malpighi (1628–1694), the first to use a microscope to study anatomy, depicted the capillary systems of humans. In an attempt to find out whether frogs originated from eggs or by spontaneous generation, Malpighi reconstructed the stages of a frog's embryological growth. He dissected the silkworm, producing the first monograph on an invertebrate; pioneered insect anatomy; and offered classic accounts of the germination of bean, laurel, and date palm. Nehemiah Grew (1641–1712) added sex to microcosmic life. He guessed that flowers are the sexual organs of plants and observed that pollen grains—those most precious dusts—"are the body which bees gather and carry upon their thighs."[34] The work of Jan Swammerdam (1637–1680), a marvelous dissector and illustrator, was collected in his *Bible of Nature*, which is considered "the finest collection of microscopical observations ever produced by one worker." In his *Bible* he depicted an anatomy of the bee, the spore cases of ferns, and the developmental stages of gnats, dragonflies, and tadpoles.

Anthony van Leeuwenhoek (1632–1723) was the most famous of the microscopists. He used the best lenses ever made and reserved the finest of his microscopes for his eyes alone. Magnifying objects 270 times, an accomplishment unrivaled for nearly two centuries afterward, he caught glimpses of bacteria and offered the first descriptions of red blood cells, protozoa, and other unicellular organisms. He furnished a keen description of an insect's eyes and sketched the development of the ant, the spinning and poison apparatus of spiders, and the metamorphosis of the flea. Leeuwenhoek literally brought into view for the first time new kingdoms of life. Dust would never again be so simple.

In one of the crucial steps in science's definition of the minuscule, Robert Hooke (1635–1703), investigating the structure of cork, discovered and defined cells. Hooke explained the minute stinging apparatus

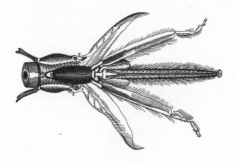

*Swammerdam's mouth parts of a
honeybee, ca. 1675*

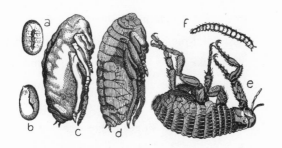

*Leeuwenhoek's development of a flea.
(a) Egg. (b) Eggshell after escape of
larva. (c) and (d) Stages of pupa.
(e) Young complete insect. (f) Larva.*

Hooke's microscope

of nettles and, further discriminating among dust's associates, depicted the growth of mosses and molds. He was the first to depict the polyzoon, a tiny, mollusk-like water animal forming branching colonies resembling brownish moss or seaweed. He also discerned the markings on fish scales, the structure of the bee's stinger, and the "tongues," or "radulae," of mollusks. Charles Singer judges the best of Hooke's *Micrographia* to be "really wonderful," especially "his figures of a gnat and its larva, of the compound eyes of a fly, and two perfectly gigantic pictures of a flea and a louse."[35] This newly discovered microcosm contained whole forests of plant and animal life.

The classical microscopists proved Pascal's intuition that the microcosm below was equal in scale and complexity to the macrocosm above. A mathematician who studied such intangibles as the equilibrium of liquids, the nature of the void, and the weight and pressure of air (sensing, as Torricelli had before him, that we live in a sea of air), Pascal (1623–1662) wrote of his intuition: "Let him see therein an infinity of universes, each of which has its firmament, its planets, its earth, in the same proportion as in the visible world; in each earth, animals, and in the last mites, in which he will find again all that the first had, finding still in these others the same thing without end and without cessation. Let him lose himself in wonders as amazing in their littleness as the others in their vastness."[36]

The Italian naturalist Lazzaro Spallanzani (1729–1799) was one of those scientists attracted to microscopic worlds even though the era's approbation was reserved for those who scanned the heavens. Spallanzani proved that the smallest living things have parents, just as Francesco Redi (1626–1697) had shown a century before that the worms in putrefying meat are the larvae of flies. Contradicting the dominant belief of preceding ages and his own, Spallanzani argued against spontaneous generation.[37] He suggested that the minutest forms of life reproduce without the influence of heavenly ether or the inherent fertility of surrounding earth or air. Spallanzani identified his discovery of the mysterious world of microbes with Christopher Columbus's discovery of the New World.[38]

At the time, no one concurred that Spallanzani's work was as great

Mites between the scales of a flea

as he thought it was. Prejudice still preferred ascents of the mind to the sublimities of the heavens rather than descents into the unseen life below. Above, God resided, and, if not God, at least a great rationale prevailed, lending glory and credence to science's mathematical mapping of the macrocosm. Better one deity who made clocks than swarms of tiny, teeming inhabitants of dust, air, and water. Even Jonathan Swift seemed to demean the microscopists of the era when he wrote:

> So naturalists observe, a flea
> Has smaller fleas that on him prey;
> And these have smaller still to bite 'em;
> And so proceed *ad infinitum*.[39]

Despite such mockery, the microcosm would prove to be no laughing matter, especially when the causes and cures of disease were found within it. Microscopic pathfinders would populate the invisible with colonies of multifarious organisms that were perhaps as numerous as the sprites and hobgoblins of old and the spirits of the celestial orbs above.

STILL TRAPPED BY DUST AND DARKNESS

For the great majority of seventeenth- and eighteenth-century people, minute things still lay behind the boundaries of dust, darkness, and skin. Seeing the invisible world close up was the privilege of a few. Even those who wore the new eyeglasses saw less than we see today. The standard eyeglasses of our era—made of precisely ground lenses, mounted over both eyes, held firm behind the ears—did not exist until the end of the eighteenth century and were not mass-manufactured until the middle of the nineteenth century. Monocles, lorgnettes, magnifying glasses, pince-nez, bifocals, individual goggles, and telescopes were the devices early modern Europe used to read the small writing on a page, pick out an individual face at the opera, or scan the heavens. Although lens grinding improved, many eyeglass lenses were colored and made of quartz or beryl (the German word for beryl, *Brille,* also means glass). Like wristwatches, eyeglasses before the nineteenth century were individually made and often were works of art, with intricate cases.[40]

Surgery, which requires keen sight and fine tools, afforded a measure of civilization's precision. Surgery depended then—as it did until the twentieth century—on available daylight. Operating theaters were built with glass domes. The finest surgical instruments were by twentieth-century standards anything but precise. Though they were often ornate, with handles of carved wood, ivory, or tortoiseshell, they were not uniformly calibrated until the beginning of the nineteenth century.

(Their original makers were armorers, the most skilled of medieval and Renaissance metalworkers. Silversmiths took over until specialized instrument makers appeared in the eighteenth century.) They commonly rusted until the early twentieth century, when stainless steel was introduced.[41] In sum, the finest instruments of the age—the best tools for manipulating the delicately small—still wrench the nerves of the contemporary observer when we imagine them entering the most sensitive places of the human body.

The absence of precise instruments, the lack of knowledge, and a shortage of light, all of which limited Europeans' ability to control the small, coalesced in a horrifying incident: Johann Sebastian Bach died from surgery on his strained eyes, a condition that purportedly resulted from his copying of music.[42] Surely there would have to be greater control of the small—a great cleanup of dust and darkness—for Western civilization to avert such tragedies. More light and knowledge, and less dust and darkness, were needed to make this earth the pleasant garden men and women would have it.

CHAPTER FOUR

THE GREAT CLEANUP

> The fundamental point is not the appearance of new ideas, but the
> appearance of conditions that make such ideas relevant.
> —Maurice Agulhon, quoted in Eugen Weber,
> *Peasants into Frenchmen*

The story of Western society's rendezvous with the small and invisible
is a multifaceted story. It is about intellectual discovery and technological control of the small and invisible. It is about increasingly minute
human creations. It also concerns the majority's escape from a world
whose limits in all preceding ages were dust, darkness, and disease, and
its entrance into a world of unrivaled abundance and unprecedented
control of water and light.

The story of pushing back the borders of the small grew out of
Europe's spreading power, the advancement of knowledge, and the
perfection of manufacturing techniques. It led—as we have already
seen—to the refinement of European crafts and their capacity to shape
materials of the earth into intricate goods. It flowed out of Europe's

successful adaptation of the best Chinese and Arabic technologies. It converged with a sixteenth-century revolution in trade and production, accompanied by a dramatic increase in population; expanded agriculture, lumbering, and manufacturing; stunning advances in shipbuilding, mining, and metallurgy; and Europe's global search for goods and markets.[1] In all directions European civilization showed itself intent on occupying and controlling more space and more things.

Europe's exploration of the imagined horizons of the world merged with a mounting intellectual curiosity about the particularities of life. The Renaissance's "seemingly endless partitioning of the world"—its "delight in particularization," to use Jonathan Sawday's phrases—pervaded social and intellectual life.[2] It was stimulated and made possible by new insights and instruments. The telescope, in one direction, and the microscope, in the other, looked toward the infinite.

Europe's descent into the microcosm progressed from the factors that underlay the seventeenth-century scientific revolution, in particular, and the formation of the natural sciences, in general. These factors included scholastic rationalism's proclivity to argue about propositions as well as three models of creation: the Aristotelian notion of creation as organic and purposeful; the magical and Neoplatonic conception of the cosmos as an enigma to be deciphered; and the emerging mechanical and mathematical view of nature, which conceived of the world as a machine, a set of functions and forces that could be calculated by numbers and formulated in terms of physical laws.[3]

Yet these factors did not materially alter people's everyday relationship with the small. They did not rescue the vast majority of people from the dust, darkness, and disease that had held them since exile from the Garden of Eden. They did not provide society at large the means or materials to manipulate the small for the common good. However, the Industrial Revolution did.

The Industrial Revolution began in Britain in the last decades of the eighteenth century and spread to much of Western Europe, the United States, and Canada by the first half of the nineteenth century. It has transformed much of the rest of the world in the twentieth century. It has altered not only nature and nations and the worlds of work and production but also the minuscule things of everyday life.

The Industrial Revolution embodies a paradox. Notwithstanding the fact that it befouled and contaminated the earth's soil, water, and air, it was also the engine for an unprecedented cleanup of human beings and their societies. It permitted humans en masse to improve their dwellings and communities, freeing themselves from the old tyrannies of dust, dirt, parasites, and disease. It set the stage for a new human relationship with small and invisible things. Little things felt, smelled, and looked different, and they were utilized in new ways. The Industrial Revolution let people for the first time comprehend and control things they could neither see nor touch. The microcosm, as never before, was made pliable to human dreams.

THE BEGINNINGS OF A TRANSFORMATION

Until the Industrial Revolution, humanity accepted the cyclical nature of life. Nature's tides of composition and decomposition turned the small into the big and the big back into the small. Common sense held that over time all beings would find their way to dust and that dust itself formed a barrier between the visible and the invisible that could not be negotiated by the living.

Before the Industrial Revolution, dust held real and metaphorical powers over human experience. Humanity lacked the science and technology to differentiate minuscule entities. It also lacked the means to illuminate these small things. Things were too universally dull, so it appeared, ever to become uniformly bright.

The experience of disease provides an important example of how fundamentally human conceptions of the small would change in the eighteenth and nineteenth centuries. Carlo Cipolla has showed how even the most advanced cities in the preindustrial era lacked any effective means of maintaining public hygiene.[4] Tracing the transformation from temporary health boards to permanent magistracies in fifteenth- and sixteenth-century Italy, Cipolla has demonstrated how Italian cities went from implementing stopgap measures against epidemics to establishing long-term policies of preventive action. These policies disappeared in succeeding centuries until revived by the English and French in the early nineteenth century.[5] However, even in these most advanced Italian cities, public health measures were aimed at diseases that might develop into plagues, whose origins city officials did not understand. They did not grasp how disease spread to humans from fleas infected with the blood of a sick rat or a sick man, or how people infected by the plague could spread the disease by coughing or spitting out infected mucus.[6]

With no knowledge of microbes or disease vectors, people of earlier centuries relied on the uncontested theory of humors and miasmas of contaminated air. They mopped up dirt and dust because these led to smells, which produced miasmas, which under certain conditions could develop into pestilence.[7] Even Edwin Chadwick's influential 1842 *Report on the Sanitary Conditions of the Labouring Population of Great Brit-*

ain rested on this equation of smell and disease. Besieged by filth in every quarter, Europe and the rest of the world lived in constant fear of plague. People believed that dirty conditions (privies draining into wells and open courtyards, and heaps of animal excrement) could produce the putrid air that caused the plague.

In its earliest phases, the Industrial Revolution appeared to do nothing for human health or cleanliness. To the contrary, especially to the eye anxious for reform in the city and forgetful of conditions in the countryside, industry seemed to be creating a fouler and dustier world. Social critics, inspired by Enlightenment ideals, saw in the commotion and smoke of the new industrial city only dust and disease.

Surveys of rural and urban Britain in the first half of the nineteenth century illustrate how conditions that had once been considered normal, if not universal and preordained, now shocked the awakened sensibilities of the new elites. In 1844 in the House of Commons, Richard Cobden revealingly described the conditions of Welsh farm laborers:

> They live in mud huts, with only one room for sleeping and cooking and living—different ages and sexes herding together. Their cottages have no windows, but a hole through the mud wall to admit the air and light, into which a bundle of rags or turf is thrust at night to stop it up. The thinly thatched roofs are seldom drop-dry, and the mud floor becomes consequently damp and wet, and dirty almost as the road; and to complete the wretched picture, huddled in a corner are the rags and straw of which beds are composed.[8]

The new industrial centers were depicted as dirty and overcrowded, a refrain, heard in Macbeth's "no pure air in the cities," that had echoed since the Middle Ages. City air, critics demurred, did not free people from the tyranny of dust. Rather, life in the city meant the loss of space, fresh air, and moral uprightness. One report noted Liverpool's downward history. In 1790, 25 percent of its population lived in cellars and back houses; an 1840 survey of twenty-six streets "revealed that no fewer than 804 out of a total of 1,200 'front houses' were 'without either yards, privy, or ash pit.'" Judged in the 1840s to be "the most unhealthy town in England," Liverpool suffered a high death toll. "The mean duration for life was roughly 26 years, whereas corresponding figures for London and Surrey were 37 and 45."[9] Governed by local ordinances rather than by national laws for the first half of the century, the industrial cities were engulfed in "a putrid miasma." Because these cities had no lawns or paved roads, rains turned them into quagmires of muck.

The industrial workplace was grim and lethal. Chadwick wrote, "In some of the 'dusty trades,' the excessive amount of premature mortality is so great as to justify interference." He went on to recommend the Paris Conseil de Salubrité, whose laws demanded good ventilation; required workers to wash their hands before eating and leaving the shops; forbade them to take any meals in the shops; required "boarding off the mills and sieves, so as to prevent the escape of smaller particles"; and required workmen engaged in processes that produced lead dusts to "cover their nose and mouth with a slightly moistened handkerchief."[10]

"The 'chimney-boys' of the eighteenth and nineteenth centuries make one of the saddest chapters in the history of inhumanity," according to Lawrence Wright. In 1817, the British Select Committee heard the tragic story of a boy stuck in a chimney: "A bricklayer was got and the chimney was broke into, where the boy was found, his head surrounded on all sides by soot; he was suffocated and dead."[11]

Dirt ruled the early industrial order. At the same time, a more democratic sensibility was trying to get everyone's head up and out of the dust. Both writers who believed in reform and those who longed for the good old days depicted industry as a befouling evil. Voicing what was to become a common panegyric, John Ruskin bemoaned the abandonment of the cottage of old:

> It had been left in unregarded havoc of ruin; the garden-gate still swung loose to its latch; the garden, blighted utterly into a field of ashes, not even a weed taking root there; the roof torn into shapeless rents; the shutters hanging about the windows in rags of rotten wood; before its gate, the stream which had gladdened it now soaking slowly by, black as ebony and thick with curdling scum; the bank above it trodden into unctuous, sooty slime: far in front of it, between it and the old hills, the furnaces of the city foaming forth perpetual plague of sulphurous darkness.[12]

Dickens offered one of countless descriptions of the dirty people of this new order in *The Old Curiosity Shop*. Wandering homeless at night, the old man and Nell are approached "by the form of a man . . . miserably clad and begrimed with smoke, which perhaps by its contrast with the natural color of his skin, made him look paler than he really was." He offers them refuge, indicating a place where they "saw a lurid glare hanging in the dark sky; the dull reflection of some distant fire. 'It's not far,' said the man. 'Shall I take you there? Where you were going to sleep upon cold bricks; I can give you a bed of warm ashes—nothing better.'"[13] Ashes were the bed of the poor, dust still their daily companion.

PUBLIC HEALTH TAKES HOLD

Some attempts were made to alleviate the squalor of the new industrial cities. Alert to the danger of miasmas, and vigilant about the accumulation of waste, newly established public health organizations scrutinized the industrial order. Their officials tended to be members of the upper classes, which identified disease with the working class and the excrement that poured from the slums. In the course of the century, Alain Corbin suggests, the upper classes became "the olfactory police of society."[14] They were the conscience and sensibility of the great cleanup.

But to tell the story of the great cleanup as that of a single class, or even a single era, ignores the continuity of Western history. Public water supply and sewage disposal had occupied the attention of Greek, Roman, and medieval civilizations, as well as certain Renaissance cities like Urbino.[15] As the Industrial Revolution progressed, Europeans gained the tools to distance themselves even farther from dust. Cleanliness became a matter of good manners. Wearing clean clothes and shoes elevated a person. Escaping the muck and manure was a worthwhile goal.[16]

In the eighteenth century, civic authorities had begun to regulate water and waste and to enforce public health measures to prevent epidemics. The middle class on both sides of the Atlantic was intent on being comfortable at home and in the coffeehouse.[17] Attempts to improve society were under way in many sectors. They involved improving commerce, stimulating trades and crafts, building roads and digging canals, consolidating laws, systematizing punishment, and reforming government. Taking their cue from the spreading spirit of reform, eighteenth-century utopian thinkers imagined a populace that was educated, ordered, and something other than coarse and stinking.[18]

Reforms, both material and moral, spread throughout the nineteenth century as the means to control dust and disease grew. Official weights and measures continued to replace traditional ones; trails were superseded by roads, which gave way to the railroads. Political heroes vied with priests and saints. Banking systems, public education, newspapers, and the military draft lined up men and women and marched them, body and soul, into the future. Nineteenth-century Europe transformed its peasants into national citizens.[19]

Reformers had a mission to purify society and clean it up. For the most zealous, this meant attacking dirt on all fronts: undoing filthy peasant ways; combating "the dark and bloody" legacy of the Middle Ages; waging war against the unjust and arbitrary rule of tradition; and taking on, bit by bit, all that was filthy and corrupt. Attacking dirt meant nothing less than whisking aside all impediments that stood in the way of humanity's potential. The Enlightenment ideal, a symbiosis of moral and material good, directed humanity toward an entirely new order.

The great cleanup was not simply a matter of ideals; it was also a matter of means. At the same time that the Industrial Revolution was creating unprecedented amounts and types of dust, it provided a host of devices and agents to make the world spotless.

Industrialists, if they did anything, turned nature to dust. From mining to lumbering, steelmaking to printing, industrialists created new dusts as they transformed the earth's materials. With steel plows and gasoline tractors, dredges and ditchers, they opened the earth to the winds. The production and consumption of that age are recorded by dust accumulated in the depths of the sea, in the polar ice caps, and at the outer limits of the atmosphere.

Paradoxically, as industrial society kicked up dust, it also mounted an arsenal of tools and chemicals for cleaning up bodies, homes, and cities.[20] It mass-produced brooms, brushes, shovels, feather dusters, scouring pads, soaps, and caustic sodas. Humans shaped the landscape to fit their purposes with the help of dynamite, cranes, road graders, and bulldozers, which kicked up incredible amounts of dirt. For the home, there appeared the Bissell carpet sweeper and vacuum cleaner (which in its early forms redistributed dust as efficiently as it swept it up). For yards, lawns, and streets, there were mowers and hoses. And standing at the forefront of this arsenal was the almighty water pump, which brought in water to remove dust, dirt, and waste—and also removed stagnating or flooding water. The pump was already "a symbol of salvation in seventeenth-century England, for it was not only the answer to flooded mines but it enabled water to be brought to the towns and removed from potential agricultural land."[21]

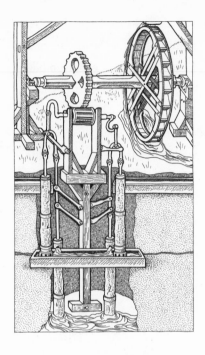

A suction pump in a mine driven by water, ca. 1561; future generations' pumps would later transform the English landscape.

The mass manufacture of clothing enhanced personal cleanliness and fastidiousness.[22] Improvements in food processing and packaging freed stores and homes of the bits of food, blood, flies, and rancid smells that evoked the slaughterhouse and the farm. In the 1890s, the Germans produced detergent, a soap of molecules that did not combine with the salts in hard water and could be rinsed away, and shampoo, a soap that removed grime and oil from the hair with one type of molecule and was washed away by another.[23]

Once introduced, the array of cleansers and cleaning agents, dyes and paints grew with the spread of industrial society. These were the first products of the modern chemical industry, whose growth accelerated from the 1880s onward.[24] These products made manifest chemistry's capacity to transform the raw materials of the earth into agents for purifying and coloring the world. (They also reinforced the modern predilection to equate optimism with light and color and pessimism with darkness and dirt.)

Brand names became society's vernacular language of cleaning as innovative cleaning instruments and products redefined everyday life.[25] A number of today's largest companies originated with everyday goods serving the great cleanup. In 1806, Colgate-Palmolive began concentrating exclusively on selling candles, soap, and starch. Procter & Gamble, a candle and soap company founded in 1837, flourished in the 1870s with the hiring of its first chemist and the subsequent creation (in part accidental) of a white soap that carried it to the forefront of the soap industry. In 1882 Samuel Curtis Johnson started selling wax to care for the parquet flooring he sold in his Racine Hardware Company. The wax became nationally known as Johnson's Wax. In 1886 another Johnson, a New England druggist, inspired by Joseph Lister's discovery that airborne germs were the source of infection, joined his brother in producing sanitized wound dressings. They started by making a medicinal plaster but soon produced a soft, absorbent cotton gauze dressing. Thus was born Johnson & Johnson. In 1888, to take an example that joins cleaning and beautification, a young entrepreneur, David H. McConnell, observed that his customers preferred his promotional perfumes to his books. (This is, perhaps, the discovery every author makes sooner or later.) What McConnell brewed in his pantry and sold successfully door-to-door became the first products of the Avon Corporation.[26] One morning in 1895 another ambitious traveling salesman,

Soap advertisement, ca. 1900

annoyed by his dull straight razor, came up with the idea of the disposable razor. Six years later, with the help of an educated machinist, he created the American Safety Razor Company, which eventually became the Gillette Company.

This list of inventions suggests that the history of the great cleanup does not rest solely with reformers and housewives. It turns on technology and business, whose protagonists, almost exclusively men, are associated with tool design, new energy sources (especially the perfection of the steam engine and the gasoline motor), metallurgy, and new construction materials.

The history of the vacuum cleaner is a part of the story of the great cleanup that recent feminist histories of cleaning have ignored.[27] This history amounts to 150 years of male inventions aimed at battling dirt and dust on pavement, floor, and carpet. It runs from giant, portable, street vacuum machines and clumsy carpet sweepers with brushes, to impossibly heavy home vacuum cleaners, to today's diversified host of lightweight electric cleaners that suck up stones and water as well as dust. It involves forgotten names like Booth and Booth (Englishmen), Herricks (an American), McGaffey (the first person to patent a non-electric, straight-suction vacuum), Bissell (a Grand Rapids, Michigan, man with an allergy to straw dust), Dufour (a woman who, in 1902, held an early patent on a primitive vacuum cleaner), and Spangler (a Canton, Ohio, janitor whose severe asthma drove him to invent an electric vacuum cleaner). Spangler visited his cousin, Mrs. William H. Hoover, who interested her engineering- and business-minded husband in producing the machine. Hoover became president of the new vacuum cleaner company in 1908, with Spangler as superintendent. This history also includes inventions that should rightly be forgotten, like the "vacuum powered by a bellows connected to a rocking chair. The idea was that the man of the house could enjoy the evening paper rocking in the chair while his wife performed the vacuuming."[28]

WATER, LIGHT, AND OTHER ELEMENTS OF THE GREAT CLEANUP

The Industrial Revolution's contribution to the great cleanup can be understood under five rubrics: new goods; new materials; dirt- and water-resistant surfaces; water control; and lighting.

The new goods took many forms. They ranged from the plastic toothbrush, floating soap, and shoe polishes to street cleaners and packaged and frozen food. Frozen foods followed the triumph of the refrigerator and freezer over the icebox in the 1930s and 1940s. Along with more packaged and canned foods, frozen foods meant cleaner stores and homes, as kitchens, yards, and basements saw fewer rotting vegetables, leaking barrels, and rusting cages, and less killing of animals. However, all the new packaging generated wastes of another kind, suggesting a law of the great cleanup: as dust and dirt are banished, waste and garbage multiply.

Beginning with the mass production of cotton clothing, the Industrial Revolution produced a parade of synthetic fabrics, including nylon and rayon. These fabrics proved easier to care for than wool. The clothing industry, which killed its share of animals for leather and fur, colorfully dressed the masses in cheap clothes and shoes. The mass production of underclothing became highly profitable: in 1868, British manufacturers reported making a million pounds selling three million corsets.[29] Not to be outdone, French manufacturers succeeded in putting the vast majority of women in France in underpants. The chemical industry not only created new fabrics for clothes, bedding, and curtains but also produced blemish removers and dyes for them.

With new materials chemists also created new surfaces.[30] Brighter, smoother, more resistant to heat and less permeable to liquids, these surfaces were less hospitable to dust and dirt. Concrete, cast iron, steel, aluminum, chrome, oilcloth, rubber, plastic, Bakelite, vinyl, and Teflon formed the fresh, shiny, and colorful surfaces among which Western urbanites began to live and work.[31] Linoleum (produced in England in 1860 and in the United States in 1925) and other synthetic floor coverings made floors easier to clean. Plaster provided smoother walls; cheaper paints and wallpaper covered cracks and created cleaner, more colorful rooms. Eventually, even basement walls made of fieldstone were replaced by brick, block, and poured concrete. These new materials could be used to create spaces in which dust and grime accumulated less easily, and they also lent themselves to easier cleaning. The housewares revolution, which has transformed the kitchen and the bathroom in this century, hinged on new materials and their shiny surfaces.[32]

Floor coverings became common. With rugs, which had been scarce, people could make their dwellings comfortable and intimate—the sort of place we have come to call home.[33] (Doubtless, rugs' initial function of keeping the dirt down on earthen floors did not produce the pristine effect contemporary carpets do.) Then, around 1900, new floor-covering materials began competing with carpeting. Their promoters accused rugs of "corrupting the air by retaining impure gasses, hiding the finest and most penetrating dusts beneath them, while giving off particles of fine wool in the atmosphere." A Pennsylvania interior decorating and artistic wood-floor company, using what would become a standard attack against carpeting, asserted that "the better grades of carpet are mixed with cow's hairs, shoddy and other unwholesome materials," providing a possible haven for infectious "microbes and bacilli that float in the atmosphere."[34]

To complement these new surfaces, the chemical industry developed a range of new paints and protective coatings. In 1804, chemists created white lead, an important pigment for paint that enabled industrial society to cover the cracks and edges of a rough world. The first varnish was sold in 1815; the first ready-made paint was available in 1867; and nitrocellulose quick-drying lacquer appeared in 1923. Quick-drying phenols, paints, and lacquers made from new chemical bases appeared throughout the 1940s and 1950s, further helping humanity transform the surfaces of its world.

One of the most important tools in the Industrial Revolution's cleaning arsenal was water, earth's first cleanser. New metals, rubbers, and plastics enabled humanity to drill, pump, and pipe great quantities of water. It was conveyed efficiently across immense distances and through tight spaces. Unlike the irregular stone channels used since antiquity and the hollowed-out logs that formed London's water main in 1721, cast iron, steel, and cement pipes formed ideal conduits for large volumes of water. Inside homes and business places, copper pipes and rubber and plastic hose proved excellent new vessels for water.

The technologies of modern plumbing turned water into a docile agent and a powerful ally.[35] In city and countryside, water control went hand-in-hand with control of the land. Drainage and irrigation leap-frogged their way across modern history. Water made fields fertile and cities and homes comfortable and hygienic. Discussing Victorian cities in England, Asa Briggs remarked, "Perhaps their outstanding feature was hidden from public view—their hidden network of pipes and drains and sewers, one of the biggest technical and social achievements of the age, a sanitary 'system' more comprehensive than the transport system."[36] David Pinckney judged Paris's Second Empire sewage system to be one of the engineering triumphs of the nineteenth century. It contributed to the decisive decline of waterborne disease in Paris and allowed the Parisians of 1900 to say "Adieu ville de boue" (good-bye, muck city), as Jean-Jacques Rousseau allegedly once bid farewell to the city he so admired and hated.[37]

In the United States, improvements in cleanliness and sanitation depended on political and regulatory changes. New York waited until the 1840s for a wholesome supply of public water.[38] Such systems depended on new technology, such as giant pumps and cast-iron pipes.[39] Cast-iron pipes were first used for four hundred feet of Philadelphia's waterworks in 1817; as late as the 1840s Detroit, a city eventually known for its great waterworks, still used hollowed tamarack logs to convey water. While hundreds of cities had installed waterworks by the 1870s, Joel Tarr indicates that few of them constructed sewer systems because it was believed that the technology was unnecessary, unproved, or too costly.[40]

By the end of the century, with running water available in schools and hospitals, dirt and dust had lost their hold on society. Thanks to the availability of public water, washing the great unwashed became a possibility, a practicality, and a mission, as Marilyn Williams suggests in her history of the public bath in urban America.[41] By 1950, when faucets and toilets had entered the great majority of homes in the Western world, the most humble residents of this century had surpassed in salubrity and comfort the aristocrats of Versailles a mere two centuries before.[42]

But before people could clean themselves and their world, they had to realize just how dirty they were. They had to perceive grit and grime and discern the source of foul odors. They needed light, the fifth important tool of the great cleanup.[43] By the end of the eighteenth century, Londoners considered street lighting a matter of public safety. Now depicted as the most reactionary of nineteenth-century popes, Pius IX was considered quite progressive when he introduced streetlights in Rome in 1846. Light turned night into day—and with that transformation came the improvement of the Eternal City and the promise of reforming darkness itself. In lighted cities, people could shop, stroll, and play after dark.[44] Criminals and unsavory elements, like dust and dirt themselves, could no longer lurk in shadows. According to the French thinker G. Bachelard, "we live in the age of administered light."[45]

Lighting opened roads, aided in navigating ships, provided beacons and traffic signals to regulate civilization's movements, and lengthened the workday. Headlights appeared on cars and trains. Electrification, which became widespread in the 1920s and 1930s, spelled the end of night's blackness—and banished countless inhabitants of the dark. With the single flip of a switch the world of the past vanished.

Light enhanced the shine of the new goods and surfaces. Gas and electric lighting did away with the soot of torches, candles, and fires. Attics, basements, and closets no longer harbored darkness and dirt. Gas stoves were lauded not only for reducing the time and labor of food preparation but also for freeing cooks from the frequent disposal of ashes and cinders from coal and wood stoves.[46] Light brought out colors vividly. It made new metals and alloys (especially chromium, steel, and aluminum) shine and plastics and enamels glow.

As a corresponding preference developed for bright interiors, transparent glass—now machine-made, colored, more homogeneous, nonconductive, and highly resistant to weathering—became all the more popular.[47] Glass windows appeared in more and more homes and businesses. Countless photographs from the beginning of the twentieth century depict a merchant and a small group of salespeople, dressed in their best, standing before shining glass cabinets in what appear to us now to be dark and cluttered rooms. Glass doors in cabinets and buildings and glass windows in stores, trains, and cars permitted the world to look in and out at itself. Glass (and later transparent plastic) bottles, jars, and showcases displayed the goods of an abundant society. Cellophane too later played its part in creating a see-through world.

The large-scale manufacture of standard eyeglasses—made increasingly of glass rather than quartz—in the second half of the nineteenth century equipped more people to see these bright new things. With lighted offices and the new age of physical and laboratory diagnosis, medical doctors carefully examined minutiae in and from the body and began to probe the body itself with standardized, sanitized, and more precise instruments.[48] They introduced a new regime of precision into medicine.[49] Eye doctors looked deep into the human eye, while surgeons threw as much artificial light on their patients' innards as they could. Theater lights shone on actors and opera singers as never before.

With light at its service, nineteenth-century society could boast about every clean new surface. The Crystal Palace, built in Hyde Park, London, for the Great Exhibition of 1851, was the highest expression of the era's architectural progress. It was made of an amount of glass equal to a third of England's total production in 1840 and was a fitting declaration of the confidence of a commercial civilization willing to say, "Let light shine upon our wares."[50]

The Industrial Revolution's creation of unprecedented quantities of goods, new materials, and washable surfaces further heated reformers' passion for a world without blemish. They were encouraged to take civilization's pipe-dreams seriously. Bountifully cheap soap helped. By one estimate, the use of soap increased fourfold in the nineteenth century.[51] Deodorants and other fruits of the pharmaceutical industry brought civilization a whiff of the promised land.

Beauty, hygiene, and sanitation tended to converge. Each one played an important role in making the great cleanup an interior imperative. Facts and conditions preceded imagination. But once stimulated, imagination, catapulted forward by desire and possibility, quickly outdistanced reality: All could, should, and would be pure.

WELL ON THE WAY TO BEING CLEAN AND DECENT

The transformation did not proceed by wish alone—nor was it anywhere near complete by the end of the nineteenth century. In cities, people were still jammed together. Garbage was still thrown on the streets. Running water and plumbing were still luxuries, and bathrooms were far from universal. Conditions in the countryside were also still abysmal. Villages were still enveloped by dust and mired in muck, and disease was endemic. Remote places would wait until after World War II for indoor plumbing and electricity.

Yet in city and countryside alike, the changes were obvious. In Paris, Eugen Weber notes, skirts no longer had to be picked up; cigarettes were no longer rolled by hand, and snuff was no longer used. People spat less and were less likely to use their hands for blowing their noses. There was more linen and laundering—and more handkerchiefs too. More people could count, read, and consult their watches. Each of these skills was necessary to survive in industrial society. Artificial light allowed people to extend their days for advantage and pleasure. Corrugated metal garbage cans, introduced in 1883 by order of Préfect Poubelle, added a new note to Paris's early-morning symphony. In 1894 Poubelle imposed a law that all wastewater go directly to the sewer system: *tout à l'égout*—everything down the drain![52]

In the countryside, too, life was undergoing a dramatic change. Public schools, a money economy, and banks all did their share. Visits from city cousins who had white-collar jobs showed rural villagers new possibilities. Conscripted young peasants posted to the cities learned about a world of bright lights. Politics linked rural locales to cities. Roads and trains brought streams of goods and released torrents of desire and envy. Weber notes that even though peasants might still have worn their wooden shoes *(sabots)*, by 1900 or so most people could afford a second pair of shoes to wear in town or to a *fête*. "By the 1920s and after," Weber quotes Pierre Jakez Hâelias, a Breton countryman and writer, "peasants no longer walked like their fathers. That is because they wear different shoes; the roads are tarred; there are not so many slopes."[53] The countryside was being changed by a sheer abundance of goods as Western society entered a period of "accumulation and display."[54]

Susan Hanson has charted a new rural world in the making in late nineteenth- and early twentieth-century Virginia by examining contemporary store inventories, photographs of stores, and mail-order catalogues.[55] She discovered that the agents of change were humble. People had more bedding and clothing, as indicated by increased sales of gingham, flannel, and muslin. A larger number of better brooms and decorated chamber pots further distanced people from their dusts and wastes. The cookstove and the kerosene lamp—two important factors in reordering rural life in this period—induced country people to buy more matches, chimneys, and wicks for their lanterns.[56] Manufactured brooms and brushes helped sweep away the kingdom of dust as well. Lye, washboards, and bar soaps improved washing. Screens, insect powders, fly paper, and rat poisons announced an intensified war on some of the rural world's oldest enemies. In vigorous efforts to clean up the defects of body and mind, an amazing variety of patent medicines (often laced with brandy or rum) were used against aches and pains of all types; opiates were used to treat mental disorders. At the same time, men and women showed an interest in the finer things of life by buying more banjos, books, and petticoats.

THE NEW BROOM REDISTRIBUTES DUST

Between 1865 and 1925, men and women in the countryside, though still awash in dust and dirt, looked forward to more wholesome lives. In 1900, Europeans and North Americans could expect a much higher standard of living. More and more people lived free of disease. Infant mortality rates began to drop.[57] Improvements in sanitation and water supply, involving considerable feats of engineering, reduced the incidence of typhoid and cholera. Better mother and infant care, improved hygiene and housing conditions, better nutrition, more education, and active government all converged to create a healthier environment.

Like a great broom, the Industrial Revolution swept dust into the gutters and to the margins of urban experience. Dust took on a different character. It increasingly became the soot, ash, and smoke that early industrialists declared signs of progress, rather than the soil and pollen of ages past. City dust was an irregular mix of sands from construction sites and manufactured wastes of all sorts. Along railroad tracks and in factory yards, grime and trash were as common to dust as pollen and soil were rare. Dust revealed what society made and consumed. It was increasingly mixed with metal fragments and glass shards. Foundries, factories, and construction sites produced their own specific dusts. Dust also varied from city to city, neighborhood to neighborhood, and even worker to worker. Children knew their place and their parents by their distinct dusts.[58]

Throughout the nineteenth century and well into the twentieth, industry produced extraordinary volumes of dust that fouled the earth, water, and air. Reviewing B. W. Clapp's recent *Environmental History of Britain since the Industrial Revolution*, J. R. McNeill noted: "The waters of the river Calder (tributary to the Humber) could be used as gray ink in the 1860s; and . . . in the same decade urchins routinely amused themselves by setting fire to the waters of the Bradford Canal. In 1936, the waters of the Trent were lethal to all animal and plant life for a stretch of 130 miles."

Nevertheless, in the next sixty years in the West, a lot of old-fashioned dusts nearly vanished, along with many of their sources: unregulated manufacturing, defecating horses, open sewers, and unpaved streets gave way to a cleaner and more orderly time. Once the common stuff of everyday life, dust was vanishing from the city as the peasant was from the new industrial democratic life.

Dust no longer defined the small, and the small was no longer coincidental with dust. In the twentieth century, the finite became a matter of atoms and microbes—and human control of them. The great cleanup prepared for humanity's encounter with these hitherto unseen entities. The Industrial Revolution, which provided society with the tools to mop up and sanitize the world, turned humanity's gaze inward and downward toward things unseen.

CHAPTER FIVE

ATOMS AND MICROBES

NEW GUIDES TO THE SMALL AND INVISIBLE

> For the infinitely little is equivalent to the infinitely great.
> —Maurice Maeterlinck, *The Life of an Ant*

> If a drop of water were magnified to the size of the world, the atoms in it would be about as large as cricket balls.
> —Lawrence Bragg, "The Atom," *A Short History of Science*

> We share the world with an incredible vast host of invisible things.
> —A. L. Baron, *Man against Germs*

In the twentieth century, smallness and dust have diverged. We have found new invisible orders in the world and within the human body, and our hopes and fears, our industry and society, have increasingly centered on these invisible entities. Two of the most powerful are atoms and microbes, discovered in this century to have the force that medieval peoples attributed to the heavens—and more. They have preempted dust as the primary representative of the small, and, in turn, have differentiated and defined dust particles.

ON THE WAY TO IO^{-16}

At the start of the twentieth century, few people in Western civilization thought, or even knew, about atoms. The newly emerging intellectual orders of the unseen had not reached the public's attention, much less become objects of interest. Even if some people could have grasped that 10^{-1} second (one-tenth of a second) is an eye blink, what would they have done with the notion that 10^{-23} second is the time it takes a photon, a particle of light, to cross the nucleus of an atom?[1]

The speculations of the first-century Roman atomist Lucretius were generally as remote to the world of 1900 as they were to his own time. Few people would have found the poetry in his *De rerum natura*—that lyric of "[the] nature [which runs] ever by unseen bodies," those "sightless bodies sweeping through / The sea, the lands, the clouds, along the sky, vexing and whirling and seizing all again."[2] Lucretius's theory contradictorily and anthropomorphically had atoms swerving from their unalterable courses to preserve human freedom. His primary intent was to regularize the events of nature and thus dispel the powers and deeds of abundant and fickle gods.

Evidently, Lucretius himself was not consoled, for blaming events not on gods but on atoms merely transferred responsibility for human misery from heaven to an insupplicable atomic microcosm. Indeed, Lucretius concluded *De rerum natura* with a dark description of the great Athenian plague: those who tended the sick quickly found themselves numbered among the dying. And so "death followed death," stacks of bodies filled the villages, and dead parents lay upon dying children. In the cities, to which dying villagers flocked, piles of bodies were concentrated around fountains and hallowed shrines of the nonresponsive gods. "The whole nation," Lucretius concluded, "was beside itself with terror."[3] What consolation was it to know that atoms had caused all this without acting in malice?

No one then—or now, for that matter—would wish to embrace such unapproachable entities. Men and women are never keen to embrace a science that teaches that, to quote Tennyson, "the stars . . . blindly run."[4] Nevertheless, as the nineteenth century progressed toward the twentieth, science turned to the little to explain the big. The main steps in its descent into the atomic microcosm were Priestley's discovery of oxygen, Boyle's work on gases, Lavoisier's triumphant use of chemical measurement, Dalton's atomic chart, and Mendeleyev's definition of the periodic table. Dalton said that the "one great object" of his *New System of Chemical Philosophy* was "to show the importance of ascertaining the relative weights of the ultimate particles, both of simple and compound bodies."[5]

In the closing decades of the nineteenth century, the atom—the indivisible kernel, the nut that could not be cracked—started to break open. In 1895, William Roentgen discovered the X ray. In 1896, A. H. Becquerel discovered radioactivity in uranium. In 1897, J. J. Thomson discovered the electron. In 1898 Marie and Pierre Curie discovered polonium and radium, having laboriously isolated one gram of radium salts from eight tons of pitchblende. Together Becquerel and the Curies showed that particles emanated from "the indivisible atom" in the form of radioactivity.

These discoveries gave birth to nuclear physics and to a whole new microcosm. The scale of this miniature world is represented by the discovery of the hydrogen atom, which has a diameter of 10^{-10} meter, and the atomic nucleus, a mere 10^{-16} meter across. From there, physicists in the late twentieth century have moved on to subatomic particles, measured at 10^{-30} meter, and even smaller entities. Today physicists investigate "things" that have no mass at all and occupy no space.

For the physicists of this century, nothing seemed too small to be divided, except perhaps the electron. And what is this nodule of existence but a tiny bit of negatively charged energy? Physicists attempted to cut in two everything they encountered. They continually asked, what is below the bottom? If traveling inward to the realm of 10^{-16} meter were equal to traveling 10^{16} meters in space, the distance traversed would equal traveling to the sun and back 3,250 times. Another measure of the nuclear physicists' microcosmic adventure was this mind-stopper: In a thimble there are statistically estimated to exist a million trillion trillion trillion (10^{42}) electrons at any one moment—and you still can get your thumb in there.[6]

In *The God Particle*, Leo Lederman writes of trendy physicists who have left behind such "established entities" as the proton and neutron. These proponents of "superstring theory" hypothesize the existence of a new breed of particles less than 10^{-35} meter across.[7] One of these particles is too subtle in movement and size to identify; another, the rarest and heaviest of all, scientists hypothesize has not existed in nature since a fragment of a second after the Big Bang, which gave birth to it fifteen billion years ago. In 1994, science celebrated the discovery of this rare mother particle, called the top quark (the term *quark* was supposedly taken from James Joyce's *Finnegans Wake*).[8]

This unseen world is anything but predictable. In contrast to the old materialist model of the atomic world, which posited matter as a bunch of billiard balls moving around empty space and occasionally bumping into each other, this new realm of the invisible is complex, diverse, and subtle, its form and motion often indicated only by faint and ephemeral traces recorded on the most refined machines and then statistically generalized. Edward Harrison speculates, "A particle . . . is a vibrant creature of a little world made cunningly."[9]

As Harrison's quote indicates, physicists often resort to metaphor to convey a sense of a universe too complex to be described accurately in anything but the most complex and arcane mathematical language.[10] Stephen Hawking has popularized the existence of black holes, caused when a star collapses in on itself under its own gravitational force and condenses to zero volume.[11] Hawking has more recently argued that black holes somehow "leak." Thus it could be said that something does come from nothing after all. The abstract, elemental, and paradoxical poetry of all this cannot be missed. In fact, Niels Bohr argued that poetry is required "when it comes to atoms."[12]

Yet for the first half of this century, the language of physics remained the domain of the few. Most people heard no celestial song in the atom's spin or in energy's dance. They had no appreciation for the subatomic discoveries of Thomson, Roentgen, Becquerel, the Curies, or Ernest Rutherford, though these discoveries made possible such popular innovations as radio and television. The atom as an object of theory or a subject of metaphor could easily be ignored. In fact, perhaps the whole galaxy of atoms held less interest than a single ant-hill, which, as Maeterlinck observed, contains a replica in secret of our human ways and destiny.[13] But the results of contemporary physics could not be ignored forever. In the words of Charles Gillispie, "Physics is power. It is education. It is war. Materially at least, it holds all things for all men, the hope or the end of the world."[14]

The importance of the atom abruptly entered the world's conscious-ness with the flash of the two atomic bombs the United States dropped on Japan in 1945. The hermetic power of the atom became blindingly visible. It was manifested in the devastation the bomb wrought, the surrender it brought about, and the nuclear arms race it engendered. Even without knowledge of all the dangers and uses of radioactivity, the public was forced to ponder the might of the atom. Something immense had come from something tiny. Even boys and girls in grade school in the 1950s learned the symbol for radioactivity and began to argue whether chain reactions have an end.

GERMS: THE INVISIBLE ENEMY

If the atomic bomb offered a rapid education in the powers of the small, germ theory had already begun to teach people that particles invisible to the unaided eye can cure and kill. Germ theory held that every-thing—from the largest organ to the dust on the head of a pin—was teeming with microorganisms. Germs altered people's sense of what inhabited the unseen worlds around and within their own bodies.

For biologists and medical professionals, germ theory opened up a rich and intriguing world and new possibilities for understanding dis-ease and its treatment. The dark side of germ theory was that all living tissue was seen as a permanent battleground between microorganisms—from parasites and bacteria to viruses and phagocytes (cells that engulf and digest other cells)—and every part of the biological kingdom was the dining table of another part.

Germ theory laid to rest the notion of spontaneous generation, which had ruled since Aristotle. People realized that frogs were not spawned

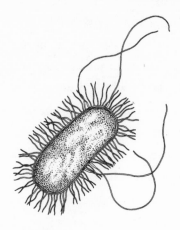

Escherichia coli *bacterium*

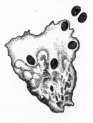

Phagocyte engulfing, ingesting, killing,
and digesting bacteria

out of marsh mud, eels from river water, worms from the soil, or flies from rotting meat. Germ theory replaced the notion of spontaneous generation with microscopic creatures that ate, strove, and reproduced. Germ theory extended the kingdom of life into the invisible.

Before the discovery of germs, doctors could view the human body, but disease and its effects on the body remained a matter of conjecture. Laboratories and diagnostic techniques did not exist. Tests and instruments were few. Hospitals were rife with infections. Surgery was performed in appalling conditions. At its best, it was carried out in the natural light of a surgical theater, but the trip to or from that theater, often located on the top floor, probably killed a good share of patients.

Ignorance abounded. Howard Haggard reports that Pierre Bayle (1647–1706) queried whether transfusions between humans would change temperament and whether transfusion of sheep's blood to a dog would ultimately turn the dog into a sheep. An early German surgeon proposed to use transfusion as a means to reconcile the parties of an unhappy marriage.[15]

Of course, investigation of the inner workings of the body had intensified from the late seventeenth century on. Battista Morgagni (1682–1771) emphasized the need for the pathological study of tissue.[16] Xavier Bichat (1771–1802) distinguished twenty-one types of tissue and linked them to functions of the body.

Cells, first identified by the early microscopists, became the microcosm of living organisms in the nineteenth century. Mathias Schleiden (1804–1881), Theodore Schwann (1810–1882), and Rudolph Virchow (1821–1902) argued that disease did not originate in the body as a whole, or even in a particular organ or tissue, but within a single cell.

Schleiden, a professor of botany, announced in 1838 that "the cell is the basic living unit of all plant structures" and directed botanical work away from classification of plants toward the study of individual plants and plant embryology. In 1839 Schwann extended cell theory to the animal kingdom. "There is one universal principle of development for the elementary parts of organisms, however different, and this principle is the formation of cells." He conceived of life itself as starting from a single cell and developing from the formation of other cells.[17]

Early microbiology was supported by a number of developments in the nineteenth century. Microscopes became commonplace in laboratories. Anatomy improved dramatically, thanks in part to the abundant maimed bodies and cadavers provided by the Napoleonic battlefields. Dissection became so widespread that people feared the poorhouse primarily because they dreaded ending up as a cadaver on the slab of a young, ambitious surgeon.[18] Anesthesia demonstrated the power of invisible gases to relieve pain and permit longer and more intricate surgical operations. Needles and syringes (originally designed by Pascal for scientific purposes and popular with Molière's doctors) became important medical instruments. A variety of endoscopes, used to observe interior canals and hollow organs, became standard tools. For example, the speculum—a small mirror fixed to the end of a rod that was illuminated from a distance by a candle—was used to study the internal cavities of the body. The ophthalmoscope was used to peer into human eyes. The two-ear stethoscope (refined by Joseph Skoda around 1840) was used to listen to the body's sounds. The S-shaped sigmoidoscope, an illuminated tubular instrument, was used to examine the rectum, while rectal cystoscopes and bronchoscopes allowed other intrusions into the body.[19]

Edward Jenner's success with vaccination gave England and Europe a convincing display of medicine's power to manipulate the unseen. (The Chinese had known about vaccination for centuries.) Jenner used benign cowpox to provide immunity against deadly smallpox—as contagious and deadly a killer as Europe had known.[20] Jenner demonstrated that people could be saved from death by the very sword that sought to kill them: a little dose could do great good.

Other insights pointed medicine toward microscopic worlds. It was observed that minute parasites and fungi caused diseases. Some microbes were shown to thrive in vomit; others were shown to cause ringworm. Long before Joseph Lister developed his antiseptic, a nineteenth-century Viennese doctor named Ignaz Semmelweis proved, though his contemporaries were not convinced, that "childbed fever can be spread from one patient to another by the very doctors who are trying to cure it."[21] Medicine had progressed a long way in mapping the dark coast of disease and infection when two explorers, the Frenchman Louis Pasteur and the German Robert Koch, changed the way we would probe the landscape of the invisible.

For his lifelong battle to understand and battle microorganisms, Louis Pasteur (1822–1895) became a national hero. His early chemical studies led to his 1848 discovery of molecular dissymmetry, which opened the door to his influential work on fermentation. His subsequent research on bacteria refuted the centuries-old theory of spontaneous generation. Pasteur matched this theoretical reach with practical innovations that aided vintners and brewers with controlling fermentation, supported silkworm breeders in their battle against silkworm diseases, and helped chicken farmers combat chicken cholera. His vaccination techniques were used successfully against anthrax and even the dreaded rabies.[22] In effect, germ theory, pioneered by Pasteur, offered clear lines of attack against invisible foes.[23] It offered both legitimacy and direction to the emerging cadres of hygienists, sanitary engineers, surgeons, and military doctors.

Germ theory defined the precise effects of diseases on tissues and organs; it described their passage from one living creature to another; and it permitted the possibility of a complete narrative of contagion, epidemic, and plague. In doing all these things, it transformed the popular understanding of unseen and minuscule things. It identified new enemies—bacteria, viruses, yeast, and fungi—and altered the common perception of small things, including dust. In particular, Pasteur's theories led the public away from generalities about dirt and dust and focused its attention on the germs that inhabited them.

Robert Koch (1843–1910) was a younger man than Pasteur and a great microscopist. Armed with a new substage illumination technique invented by Ernst Abbe and a substage condenser made by Zeiss, a German design firm, and using new techniques to stain his samples, Koch peered into the world of bacteria as no one had before. In 1884 Koch identified the source of cholera, which had a long history of terrorizing humans.[24] He traveled to Egypt after its 1883 epidemic and returned to Germany with specimens "not of poison gases, not of soils or waters but of a comma-shaped germ." It, he was to prove, caused cholera.[25] In 1882 Koch extracted the germs of tuberculosis from a diseased body. He separated them from other germs and devised a test-tube culture nutrient in which they could grow. Then he injected the germs into guinea pigs and sprayed the air with a fine infected mist, which the guinea pigs breathed. The animals died.[26]

Trypanosoma gambiense, *the*
protozoon that causes African
sleeping sickness

Koch also discovered the pernicious microorganisms responsible for anthrax (1876), wound infections (1878), and infectious conjunctivitis, or Egyptian ophthalmia (1883). He contributed to a better understanding of sleeping sickness, malaria, bubonic plague, and rinderpest.[27] Together Koch and Pasteur overturned perceptions and contradicted old proverbs. Their discoveries asserted, "What you don't know (and can't see) does hurt you." Germ theory prepared societies to battle invisible foes with science and chemistry. It pointed the way to a new line of cures that could be developed and manufactured in laboratories.

Other scientists, caught up in the enthusiasm generated by Pasteur and Koch, gave form to the emerging field of microbiology.[28] Turning their microscopes on dust, dirt, and darkness, they scrutinized the entire kingdom of the small. They linked disease to bacteria, protozoa, yeast, molds, insects, and other minute life forms. By 1900 the microbial causes of many of the most important diseases had been established.[29]

Spurred by germ theory, biology branched into diverse fields.

Protozoology, the study of single-celled microorganisms, deciphered the sources of dysentery, syphilis, and sleeping sickness. Entomology, focusing on the role of insects in spreading disease, established that typhus is carried by a kind of louse; bubonic plague by fleas; relapsing fever by ticks; sleeping sickness by a species of fly; and malaria and yellow fever by mosquitoes.[30] Helminthology, the study of parasitic worms, explained how certain worms caused diseases. Each of these fields played a role in penetrating the invisible and distinguishing human beings' precise enemies in the microcosm.[31] And, of course, they encouraged society to change its environment at the minutest levels.

In the same decade that physics introduced the Western mind to subatomic science, microbiology declared the existence of the smallest, most elusive and enigmatic creature of all: the virus. In 1892, the Russian bacteriologist Dmitri Josipovitch Ivanovsky discovered organisms that passed through his finest bacteria-trapping porcelain filters. Not true cells but tiny particles, viruses exist in the frontier between living and nonliving matter. Ivanovsky could not see his new discoveries. Measuring from 20 to 300 nanometers (10^{-9} meter), they are submicroscopic; that is, they elude the traditional light microscope, which can show objects as small as $\frac{1}{4}$ micron (10^{-6} meter). It took electron microscopy and the short wavelengths of ultraviolet light to bring viruses into view.

Once discovered, viruses engendered spirited debate. Their absence of cellular structure and their need to exist parasitically on living tissue led some scientists to argue that they should be considered nonliving material, even though their ability to reproduce argues to the contrary. While their definition remained in question, their significance did not.

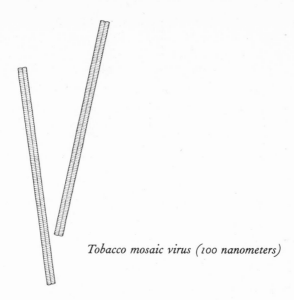

Tobacco mosaic virus (100 nanometers)

They were discovered to be the cause of many plant and animal diseases and such human killers as smallpox, yellow fever, influenza, rabies, and poliomyelitis.

Between 1880 and 1900, biologists opened the doors to microorganisms and the chambers of the cell. As modern atomists dramatically surpassed Lucretius, so modern biologists bypassed Leeuwenhoek and Hooke. They traveled the range of microscopic life and matter from cells (10^{-5} meter) to the smallest viruses (10^{-9} meter).

THE NEW DUSTS

During the first half of this century, with the discoveries of subatomic particles and microorganisms, the microcosm expanded immensely, while the macrocosm seemed to contract in the face of human power to miniaturize it. Even in physics, Einstein's theory made space seem to curve inward on itself. Though now measured in billions of light years, the universe somehow seems far less awe-evoking. Astronomers estimate that visible stars represent no more than ten percent of the total matter in the universe, yet the vastness of the universe itself originated in an explosion of the smallest and shortest-lived particles.[32]

The transformation of dust in this century illustrates this revolution of the microcosm. Once an unchallenged kingdom, dust was both a mixture and the sum of all small things. Its omnipresence was assured by the divisibility of matter. In this century, dust, like the European peasant of the old rural order, has been swept to the margins of life. It has lost its role as the first and most common measure of smallness. It is no longer a normal condition of life but a highly differentiated set of particles.

This differentiation of dust went hand and hand with scientific investigation, industrial production, and public health regulation. "It is the invisible we have to guard against," declared Robert Hessler in his 1912 book *Dusty Air and Ill Health,* which set as its goal the identification of dusts that cause diseases.[33] Fashionably, he placed dust in the framework of evolution. Before humans, there were cosmic, volcanic, desert, pollen, and animal trail dusts. With early humans there appeared dusts from tents, domesticated animals, and villages. (Somehow Hessler ignored the dusts generated by plowing, harvesting, and milling.) Next appeared "shop dust," "paved street dust," "factory dust in variety," "sidewalk dust with spittle," and "trailing dress dust," all of which correlate with such causes of illness as "large factories; crowded tenements; dusty and smoky air," and corresponding medical conditions.

In simplified terms, the absence of pure air in large cities made the contemporary period "the age of hospitals and dispensaries; one of throat and chest specialists."

As Hessler sought to associate specific sicknesses with certain dusts, Mitchell Prudden (more in accord with contemporary science) wrote in his *Dust and Its Dangers* (1903), "[Dust] is not dangerous or harmful unless among its ingredients are the living germs which come from the bodies of the persons suffering from bacterial causes."[34] Germ theory bifurcated dusts into those with and those without deadly microorganisms that ferried disease back and forth between humans and other living creatures.

Other scientists also differentiated dusts. Volcanologists, meteorologists, soil scientists, industrial doctors, and sanitarians were among the many groups of scientists who focused on different particulates. Forensic scientists solved crimes with fine dust, while archaeologists examined dusts to reconstruct the lives of earlier civilizations.[35] Production engineers refined their analysis of dusts. A 1936 text, *Industrial Dust*, underlines the importance of ascertaining the electrical and optical characteristics of specific dusts.[36] This required chemical and mineralogical analyses and the determination of particle size, velocities, and flocculation patterns. The text offered a technical discussion about dust control (with specific references to exhaust and air-cleaning systems) and considerations of dusts injurious to safety and health.

In the first half of the twentieth century, then, dust came under continuous examination. Led by universities and industrial laboratories, systematic interest in the microcosm multiplied and accelerated. Scientific disciplines divided and multiplied like the cells and molecules they studied. Industries did the same. The annual aggregate sales of measuring devices to research, laboratories, and the military would reveal the extent of the twentieth century's engagement with the small and the invisible—and suggest the identification of civilization with the control of miniature things.

Even steelmaking illustrates this conjunction. The taconite industry of Minnesota, located on the state's Mesabi Iron Range, turned on the success of a single University of Minnesota laboratory.[37] Researchers faced several complex problems. They had to find machines and processes to crush an exceptionally hard hematite ore into fine dust particles and then find a means to agglomerate and pelletize those particles into sufficiently large spheres to prevent the circulation of gases in the smelting process from blowing them—and the company's profits—up the flue.[38] Success, which took several decades to achieve, turned iron dust into army tanks in the nick of time to face Axis forces.

In peace and at war, twentieth-century industry grew more precise in its control of dusts and ultrafine materials. Chemical and pharmaceutical industries identified, manipulated, and invented molecules. One chain of molecules, called synthetic polymers, accounts for the origin of the plastics industry. Each year the United States alone makes 30 million tons of plastics, light, durable, water-resistant materials that, when translucent, can substitute for glass and make the world a cleaner, healthier, and less dusty place.

Industry's need to work with minute entities and minuscule processes spawned new industries dedicated to creating precision measuring instruments. Balances became electric, rulers gave way to micrometers, and gauges were invented to measure heat, volume (of liquids, gases, and solids), pressure, and materials.[39] Highly refined industries, the types associated with electricity and computers, have done what past ages never conceived of doing: they have dedicated entire laboratories to dust and particle control.[40] The "clean rooms" of computer laboratories have made possible what no medieval artisan had ever dreamed of: products completely free of dust.

The new laboratory tools include X rays, electron microscopes, echograms, spectrometers, and other sophisticated instruments. These machines permit entrance into heretofore unseen worlds. In laboratories, scientists engineer the invisible. They turn bacteria into cleaning agents and conjure with molecular-scale technologies.

In this world, dust has no place, unless it is assigned credentials as a specific particulate. The old kind of mixed and undifferentiated dust— the little stuff of everyday life—is now out of place. With so much known about the invisible, dust can never again be ordinary. Nor can it be considered minute when measured against the smallest entities of the new microcosm. A great divergence of dust and smallness occurred in this century when Western humanity followed the atom and the germ into more cryptic and powerful worlds.

CHAPTER SIX

DISCERNING THE INVISIBLE FOR THE GOOD OF THE NATION

> It is the invisible we have to guard against.
>
> —Robert Hessler, *Dusty Air and Ill Health*

By the end of the nineteenth century, great forces—commerce, industry, nationalism, democracy, and reform—were leading Westerners to climb the world's highest mountains, explore the deepest jungles, agriculturally transform the vast grasslands of North and South America, and trade with, colonize, and in other ways dominate the other peoples of the globe, while at home they dramatically changed their own peoples and lands. Presuming there was nothing under the sun, great or small, that they could not dominate, Western science, technology, and medicine pushed into the microcosm. The West's capacity to understand and regulate the microscopic realm established its global dominance and underlay much of its sense of superiority. With immensely expanded control over dust and germs, Western peoples enjoyed longer and better lives: in England and Wales, for example, male life expectancy rose from approximately forty years in 1850 to sixty-eight by 1950.[1] Healthier and happier peoples in turn meant stronger nations. After 1900, control of the small and the invisible became vital matters of individual rights and national well-being. The history of public health and medicine reveals how peoples of the West in the first half of the twentieth century came to adapt their lives to a new order of small and invisible things.

FIGHTING THE UNSEEN

Twentieth-century public health was defined by the previous century's mounting concern for national health and cleanliness and by the bacteriological revolution. The field of public health began to take form in the first half of the nineteenth century as a response to new movements and urban concentrations of people precipitated by the Industrial Revolution.[2] Its psychological origin lay in both a fear of the masses and a sense of responsibility for the good of society at large. This attitude on the part of the elite was enhanced by fear of and revulsion toward the dust, disorder, and disease that seemed to lurk in the poor neighborhoods of the new industrial cities and a surging optimism about realizing the most utopian Enlightenment goals of cleaning up humanity, body and soul alike. What supported this altogether unprecedented optimistic conscience—as I suggested in chapter 4—was the newfound control over water and lighting and innovative machines and materials. Also underpinning this conscience was a forest of urban pipes, cables, and wires and a thicket of rules and ordinances.

On both sides of the Atlantic, public health faced its greatest challenges in the crowded conditions of the industrial cities. There migrants were concentrated and conditions seemed darkest, dirtiest, and most dangerous. Reformers called attention to the dangers of industries and the plight of industrial society.[3] In recently formed national armies, soldiers crowded into barracks increased the possibility for epidemics. In schools, where students and germs mingled, inspectors preached that generations of disease-laden and poorly fed youth would never produce a great nation.[4] National greatness depended on reform of the smallest things, poor eyesight and head lice included.

As much as germ theory—formulated and developed in the last decades of the nineteenth century—influenced public health, it did not derail the great cleanup's effort to eradicate plain old dust and dirt. Germ theory also was not accountable for the nineteenth-century decline in infectious diseases or the decreasing mortality rate, victories that had their sources in the early sanitary reform movement.[5] In fact, the field of public health was divided between two approaches to disease. The contagionists promoted the adoption of general hygiene and the eradication of dirt because it harbored germs; the infectionists sought to stop the spread of particular germs and impose quarantines. In either case, germ theory lent the credibility of science to the field of public health.[6] It provided a spine of intellectual coherence to the diffuse and variegated theorizing about illness and to public health's eclectic body of teaching, which comprised a jumble of remedies and regulations.[7]

Germ theory supported public health officers who sought to prevent disease by regulating city housing, water, and wastes. It provided campaigners with precise targets and in some instances resulted in spectacular successes, without contradicting the expanding impulse to make objects and people dust- and dirt-free.

Germ theory did, however, let dust off the hook as the primary cause of disease. At a 1902 annual meeting of the American Public Health Association, Dr. Charles V. Chaplin, an eminent medical professor and later the author of a classic textbook on infection, described the major shift in public health in the United States from the filth theory of disease to the germ theory in these terms:

> When our honored and lamented [Walter] Reed went to Havana and discovered that yellow fever was transmitted by the bite of a mosquito, [he] drove the last nail in the coffin of the filth theory of disease. . . . It was believed that the municipality was chiefly responsible for infectious diseases. Pure air, pure water, and a pure soil was the cry. Sanitarian reform was engaged principally in protecting drinking water from organic contamination, in building sewers, in developing plumbing into a complicated and expensive art, in clearing streets, in removing dead animals, in collecting garbage and removing household rubbish, in whitewashing and repairing tenements, in the regulation of offensive trades, and the general suppression of all nuisances affecting the sense of smell. Of course, there is some truth in the idea that dirt may be the cause of sickness. . . . But with minor exceptions, municipal cleanliness is no panacea. There is no more royal road to health than to learning.[8]

Mirroring the tendency toward specialization in all of society, germ theory turned society's attention to detailed investigations of precise causes—to those nuisances that, in Chaplin's words, "clearly and directly menace health."[9] These enemies were always hidden and often eluded the finest microscopes.

Aided by germ theory, public health officials made cleanliness a matter of public morality. In *Civics and Health* (1909), William Allen defined health as "a civic obligation." He issued a call for imperative "courses in germ sociology."[10] Every schoolchild should know not only all the presidents but the story of microorganisms and communicable diseases as well. In 1912, two American authors produced an elementary school textbook titled *The Human Body and Its Enemies*.[11] In the preface they forged a stunning link between cleanliness, race, and germ theory: "The essential principle of hygiene has ever been cleanliness. The race has developed an instinctive horror of the unclean. Since the discovery of microorganisms as the causative agents of disease, however, our adherence to cleanliness has become specific and intelligent."[12] So the masses, beginning in grade school, were to be taught an official view of the small.

By World War I, a portion of the public already believed that germs were as real and as deadly as battlefield enemies. The war not only called attention to the poor health of so many of the nation's young but also focused public sentiment on the invisible legions of disease awaiting the boys from home in the strange lands where they fought. War mobilized a long list of traditional foes: typhoid, scurvy, dysentery, and venereal disease were among the first volunteers.[13] Whole nations learned what military historians had always known: war and plague are comrades in arms. Victory itself depended on health—and health depended on winning the microscopic war.

A 1917 sanitarian guide taught U.S. medical officers that their army's well-being depended on more than keeping soldiers warm and dry. Hygiene, said the guide, played an essential role.[14] The new bacteriology required not just sanitation (housing, water, and privies for the thousands) but also attention to communicable diseases and their vectors. The guide listed dangerous animals, both wild and domestic. Ships were required to guard against disease's stealthiest carrier, the rat, which was becoming in the contemporary mind an invidious animal vector, joining dust and darkness with germs and disease. The terrible influenza epidemic of 1918 and 1919, which killed twenty million people in the United States and Europe, proved that germs had signed no armistice at Versailles.

The war intensified the belief that nations were besieged by germ-carrying outsiders. In Germany after World War I, Jews, along with anarchists and communists, were judged to be not only morally corrupting but physically contaminating society. Racism took on an even more precise biological quality. The Nazis, in their obsessive quest for racial purity, medicalized their anti-Semitism. Using pseudoscientific propaganda, they depicted Jews as vectors for germs, associating them "with rats, and all that is dark, filthy, hairy, infested, and disease-laden."[15] They redefined Jews in terms of the new medical microcosm. The dawning knowledge of the small was used to serve ideology. Hate once again proved itself capable—to use an old French expression—of making an arrow out of every stick.

Throughout the twentieth century, the education Western citizens received about germs varied considerably by class, nation, and ethnicity. Popular conceptions of the small moved in and out of focus and grew dim or bright depending on the seriousness of disease and the successes of public health in combating it. With no homogenous body of knowledge or consistent legislation behind it, public health was a patchy practice.

Naomi Rogers demonstrates this variability in the case of polio at the start of the century. Public health officials vacillated in the face of this manifest killer, which evaded both scientists' microscopes and sanitarians' rules of prevention. Baffled officials reverted to familiar defenses. They called for attacks against dirt and campaigns against flies. They pushed for sanitation and quarantines, in which they prejudicially targeted the working and immigrant classes, even though epidemiological evidence indicated that these groups were largely immune. Lacking new insights, they offered useless old instructions. The state of New York as much as confessed its inadequacy on a public health bulletin board, which comprised a string of disconnected orders and concluded with a non sequitur: "A watched child is a safe child. / Swat the fly."[16]

The public responded to this confused information in contradictory ways. Parents cautioned their children about dirt and contaminated air and forbade them to swim in public swimming pools. Some kept them at home to spare them any contact with the contagion, while others sent them away to the country, where the air was cleaner. Disarmed by "this dread spectre," officials debated the relationships between air, dirt, and disease. Scientists contested the connection between illness, environment, and individual behavior. But arguments could not banish germs. The small was still a mystery—and it could be deadly.

The response to the polio epidemic foreshadowed public health strategy throughout much of the rest of the first half of the century. Officials

"Swat the fly!"

merged germ theory with older teachings about personal hygiene and cleanliness. They included in the war against dirt and dust battles against specific germs. A standard hygiene and prevention manual from 1937 sent parents and caretakers worrying and scurrying in as many directions as fear and anxiety could carry anyone locked in battle with an indiscernible enemy. Women especially fought a daily battle against dust and germs: it required attention to a very long list of things that started with nutrition and clothing, went on to exercise, and did not neglect sex and bodily excretions. In the home-front battle against disease, homeowners had to inspect lighting, heating, ventilation, and sewage systems, not forgetting eaves, troughs, and gutters. Municipalities had equally extensive duties, which required the regulation of air and water, bathing places, sewage disposal, food, and drugs, among many others.[17]

As advancing knowledge extended human surveillance and control to more and more of the small and invisible, sanitation required an inventory of everything on and in which germs could reside. The 1933 *American Red Cross Text Book on Home Hygiene and Care of the Sick* reminded readers that "the microscope has revealed the existence of innumerable little plants and organisms, so small that even millions crowded together are invisible to the naked eye."[18] Germs could lurk on and in everything. Nearly every illness or infection supposedly had its own set of germs—and who could master their names, much less their characteristics and how to prevent them? This sort of education confronted people with a microcosmic realm too vast for the mind to grasp. It required that they think and feel differently about familiar objects. But were they to carry microscopes with them to inspect every surface? Even if they did, life could not be lived hygienically in a bubble.

However misunderstood or inconsistently acted on, the truth of germ theory had taken hold. By the late 1930s a doctor could claim, "In the short span of little more than half a century, many infections which previously were formidable risks have become uncommon or rare."[19] By 1940, infectious disease accounted for only about 15 percent of all deaths in the United States. While cautious proponents suspected that new diseases would appear and that old ones would resurface, the boldest proclaimed medicine's victory. The imminent defeat of diseases that had terrorized humanity suggested that the microcosm was on the verge of being tamed.

Perhaps no twentieth-century victory seemed more decisive than the apparent elimination of tuberculosis, which had wreaked havoc throughout history and at the end of the nineteenth century was the world's most contagious, debilitating, and killing disease. In 1900, "tuberculosis was not only the chief single cause of death in the United States, the captain of the Men of Death, but it also produced an enormous amount of chronic illness and disability among the millions of its victims."[20] The disease cut across class lines, attacking the lungs of the poet, the urban worker, and the nurse and doctor who treated them. It festered in confined living quarters and literally spread as easily as breathing in and out. In advanced stages, it attacked the lungs, causing its hosts to cough up infected sputum. The bacilli within the sputum survived for a considerable time outside the body. They were then inhaled by others through the lungs, ingested with food, or even absorbed through pores in the skin.

By 1900, the work of Koch and the scientific hygiene movement promised, in theory, the imminent defeat of tuberculosis. In fact, however, twentieth-century campaigns against the disease proved anemic, emphasizing "individual responsibility while neglecting the deep-seated social and economic problems that established close links between poverty and tuberculosis."[21] Western nations adopted diverse strategies for treatment and prevention, which ranged from inoculation and injection to sanatoriums and quarantine. Even though a "large decline in mortality occurred before the introduction of specific and effective pharmacological agents were brought into play," by midcentury it appeared that public health had defeated the "white plague."[22] In the 1950s, sanatoriums closed in droves. The United States reported a 95 percent drop in the tuberculosis death rate in the first half of the century. Britain looked back on tuberculosis, the scourge of the nineteenth century, as an affliction of a bygone era. And since the World Health Organization had distributed a tuberculosis vaccine to more than fifty million children, the West's victory appeared to be shared with the world.[23]

In 1950, when the West began to sparkle cleaner than ever before, it appeared to be on the threshold of triumphing over the world's smallest killers. The experiences of the last half of the nineteenth century had elevated the public's expectations and the confidence of progressive thinkers. Sanitary measures had caused a dramatic decline in the incidence of infectious diseases, and science had made a remarkable succession of discoveries of their causes.[24] The first half of the twentieth century continued this phenomenal exploration of the concealed worlds of the human body.[25] Thanks to continuing sanitation, the apparatus of government and law, laboratories, and public health campaigns, people of the progressive nations read accounts of vanishing diseases and were offered both explanations of and cures for nature's most enduring, menacing, and baffling puzzles.[26]

It is no wonder that by 1950 medicine had won over the public. Now able to cure infections and eradicate diseases rather than merely treat symptoms, medicine had won impressive battles against invisible foes. Doctors and hospitals were curing more and killing fewer. Crusading health officials, acting like wartime mobilization boards, ordered the nation about: people couldn't spit where they wanted, they would be quarantined and vaccinated, and fluoride in the water supply would keep their teeth gleaming. Resistance to the medical model was sparse. The antivaccinationists who had fought vaccination on both sides of the Atlantic, starting before World War I, were now scattered, only a historical curiosity left to fight solitary, ineffectual skirmishes against the "bullying health regime."[27]

This enhanced sense of well-being was increased by other factors. Bright goods made out of smooth-surfaced plastic, Bakelite, and vinyl were available to the masses. Washing machines and refrigerators became standard household appliances. They revealed a mixture of converging ideologies advocating the clean, the fresh, and the healthy, and endorsing innovative materials, novel technologies, and mass manufacture and design.[28] There was a vast quantity of bright, washable clothing. Soaps and deodorants contributed to olfactory domestication of individuals and crowds. Beauty was truly more than skin deep; it went to the bones of the culture.[29] Indoor toilets and electricity reached the most remote farms. Preventive, emergency, and highly specialized medical services cast their protective net over the minds and bodies of Western people. Though dust, dirt, and germs were not entirely banished, a new microcosmic regime had been installed—and its promise was the brightest beacon of hope to ever reach the dark shores of suffering and diseased humanity.

FOLLOWING THE DOCTOR'S ORDERS

Medicine emerged as philosopher and king of this new order. Fewer people died from accidents, contagious diseases, the bite of a rabid dog (as my great-grandfather did), or a ruptured appendix (as my thirty-three-year-old Sicilian grandfather did). Open wounds, compound fractures, and severe burns were testing grounds on which doctors and pharmacists proved their control of unseen things. Their definition of the small (seen or unseen) was as incontrovertible as feeling less pain and becoming well could make it.

Given the giant reward of good health, the price of admission to the theater of modern medicine was picayune. One needed only to profess a belief in the lethal power of germs, submit to the decrees of the family doctor or specialist, follow a basic health regimen, and occasionally take a few medicines. Modern medicine required so little faith and observance of such simple rituals in return for its great promise of a less painful, happier life. Surely religions and home remedies had demanded far more of their believers and rarely offered as much in return. The only grateful and prudent thing for any half-rational person to do was to believe the medical doctrine of the hour.

Medicine's most convincing lessons about its ability to manipulate the invisible came in the form of successful surgery, relief of pain, and powerful new drugs, including antibiotics like penicillin that for the most part replaced sulfa drugs after World War II.[30] Medicine cabinets became shrines where curing powders, sprays, and liquids accumulated. The pill, a tablet of fine dust, was contemporary medicine's Communion wafer.

In the process of defining and manipulating the small and the invisible at the nexus which matters most to people—their lives and well-being—medicine indoctrinated them into a new view of their relationship to the microcosm. Medicine's basic education, complex science aside, rested on an easily assumable view of things, its first law of reciprocity being one every peasant knew: humans live off small creatures, and they live off humans. People share their lives with a range of minuscule organisms. The trick is—and this is medicine's success—to identify and kill unwanted intruders while protecting helpful entities, mainly bacteria.[31]

Nearly universally in the West, people today observe the environment and their bodies through the lens of germ theory. Dust, skin, fingernails, and bodily orifices are seen as potential sources of infection. The color or consistency of bodily discharges may reveal the presence of alien microbes within. Observable infection offers clues to the presence of invisible processes and forms the basis of medical judgments on well-being.

Our minds are populated with ideas of germs. We know that helping germs make soils rich and digestive tracts healthy. Others cause unpleasant odors. More notorious germs cause disease: mycobacteria cause tuberculosis and leprosy, staphylococci cause boils, and gonococci are responsible for gonorrhea, while spirochetes (whose biological classification is a contested subject) cause syphilis. And there are the smaller, more sinister viruses, which aside from causing the common cold may be the source of AIDS and Ebola. In the microscopic world of killers, viruses—until recently the smallest and least understood of the germs—still constitute the greatest villains of the microcosm: they parasitize everything, including the bacteria from which they were probably derived. Some can hide for long periods: the chickenpox virus can reappear as long as fifty years after infection to produce shingles.[32] And at the end of the twentieth century we face the possibility of attack by an even smaller invader, the prion, a mysterious scrap of protein associated with "mad cow disease" and related fatal conditions.

Today people understand that the greatest things depend on the smallest—and those small things are defined, even controlled, by experts. It is no longer Cleopatra's nose that determines history, so to speak, but the germs within her nose. The smallpox vaccination scar on the upper arm of nearly every schoolchild of a generation or two ago marked our initiation into science's contemporary doctrine of the small and dangerous. Surgical scars are other marks of passage into the medical microcosm. More humble rituals, like visits to doctors, blood pressure readings at the local fire station, and the purchase of pregnancy tests at the drugstore, enroll us in the medical view of the small and invisible. Each ingested aspirin testifies to an agreement about the powers of tiny things.

Medical education includes an ever more elaborate pharmacological indoctrination. As old as spit and herbs, pestle and mortar, pharmacy has created finer, more complex, and synthetic dusts. In the past two centuries, pharmacy has become a precise science focused on the use of synthetic drugs. Its fundamental stages are associated with the formation of medical chemistry, the beginnings of the pharmaceutical industry, and the formulation of germ theory. This history culminates in the second half of the twentieth century with the beginnings of immunotherapies and chemotherapies aimed at treating noncommunicable diseases and with the dawn of experimental gene therapies.[33]

Of course there is a fly in the ointment of medical wars against microbes. Outside the West, and particularly in underdeveloped regions, they have not always resulted in victories. In fact, depending on place and disease, they have frequently produced protracted stalemates and even clear defeats. As was already well known, microbes can evolve to become resistant to modern medicine's weapons. They become stronger and more deceptive precisely because of the medicines used against them. As atoms in the form of bombs proved deadly at mid-century, so germs, in the form of new diseases, terrorize us at the century's end, showing us how intractable and sinister the unseen can be. But this is getting ahead of the story. In the first half of the twentieth century, science's discovery and control of the invisible brought good to humanity—and the microcosm, which it named and commanded, became a matter of common knowledge. Public health and medicine had delivered Western civilization to a profoundly different view of small and invisible things.

CHAPTER SEVEN

LIGHTING UP
THE MICROCOSM

> The materials research community has reached a new plateau
> of unprecedented power in its ability to understand, control, and
> manipulate the world.
> —Ivan Amato, *Stuff: The Materials the World Is Made Of*

> For good or ill, we stand at the threshold of a molecular dawn.
> —B. C. Crandall, *Nanotechnology*

As twentieth-century Western civilization sought to control the surfaces of things—as the growth of lawns and gardens and the proliferation of paved roads testified—so it also strove to light them up. By the amount and type of light it could generate, the twentieth century outshone all other civilizations. Indeed, illumination emerged as arguably the most sublime of human creations. Electric lighting became a constant and dominant element of most spectacles—from illuminated bridges and skyscrapers to the neon glow of Las Vegas in the desert. Lighting—so important to leisure, arts, sports, and work—"made possible the revisualization of landscapes, filling them with new meaning and possibilities."[1]

In illuminating the desirable, lighting exposes the undesirable. Light reveals dust and dirt; it calls in on them the broom, the cloth, and the shovel. In the contemporary form of a laser beam, light finds a place in America's $75-billion-a-year cleaning industry. Bursts of light delivered by lasers are used to remove grime, rust, and mildew.[2]

Illumination has become a matter of taste and mood. If civilization lights up the streets for safety and commerce, increasingly, at home, lights are modulated to fit personal tastes and prevailing styles. In the lit-up world, small imperfections stand out; there is less room for dust and dirt. To have the surfaces appear without blemish, society conceals beneath them a maze of wires, ever smaller and finer.

Our own bodies are subject to the same brightly lit scrutiny. On cleaner human bodies, blemishes and defects are accented. In preceding centuries, scabs, birthmarks, pockmarks, and acne were too common to command attention. Human bodies were seen nude less often. There were less bathing, swimming, and washing, and fewer changes of clothes. And clothes were certainly less revealing. There were fewer windows, mirrors, or magnifying glasses, and hence less staring and peeping. Even at home—with scant lighting and heat and no bathrooms or private bedrooms—people did not indulge in prolonged nakedness and voluptuous sex.

Medicine was not equipped to recognize or treat bodily imperfections. Sores, lesions, boils, rashes, tumors, polyps, and many other defects were considered simply "natural" and went unexamined. No medical imperative insisted on checkups, and few health regimens called for air, sunlight, or bathing. The science of dermatology did not exist.

Self-examination of one's body—and one wonders how much oc-curred—was not prescribed. Medicine had not yet even diagnosed a range of nonspecific urethral infections, gonococcal and nongonococ-cal.[3] It accepted as natural and inevitable a variety of discharges from the genital organs, especially of females, originating in infections such as vaginal thrush (a fungal infection) and salpingitis (inflammation of a fallopian tube).[4]

In the twentieth century a keener and more focused beam of light fell on the human body, as it did on other surfaces. This beam, in diverse forms, explored downward and inward, ever more finely and intensely. Like the early dissectionists' blades, the contemporary beam (which in one of its refined contemporary forms is positron emission tomography, or PET) probed for the first time into the most interior tissue, which once had been considered the inscrutable cloth of God's creation. Scientists of every discipline could now examine whole orders of the infinitesimal within and around human beings, pushing the boundary of the small and the invisible still farther back.

DUST BECOMES PARTICULAR

Dust did not escape this great illumination. It lost its credentials as a simple God-given creation or the consequence of human activity. The dust that people had known for centuries shattered into a heterogeneous set of specific particulates. Under the microscope, dust was transformed into thousands of different particles, each worthy of its own legion of scientific experts.

Since the great cleanup and the revolution in technology, all sorts of dusts have been examined. Cosmic dust, reaching across the universe, has been measured in nanograms (10^{-9} gram) and even femtograms (10^{-15} gram). It has been examined by optical telescopy and calculated by elemental ratios, isotope ratios, and the tracks of cosmic rays.

On earth, dust has become a matter of both curiosity and concern. National and regional politics have turned on the causes of silicosis. Industries—from mining, quarrying, and grinding to clothmaking and grain farming—release into the air fine toxic dusts, molds, and fungi that cause respiratory diseases and over time can bring the strongest workers to a wheezing halt. Agricultural dusts have also posed dangers. Specialists have looked at the adverse effects of dust spraying, dust concentration, and bio-aerosols in swine and poultry operations; dusts' distortion of soils; dust in droughts; and the Dust Bowl's relationship to global warming.

Some of the lethal effects of dust are more immediate. In grain elevators and other industrial environments, a single spark from any source (even the tiny amount of electricity given off by the human body) can trigger an immense explosion. Between 1900 and 1955 approximately a thousand severe dust explosions occurred in the United States, killing 650 people and destroying $90 million worth of property. These dust explosions (triggered by the fineness of the dust and its content of volatile combustible matter) occurred at grain elevators, malt houses, thermal coal dryers, woodworking shops, and food processing plants. Explosions also occurred in industries involved with fertilizers, rubber, paper, sugar, cotton, pulverized coal, metals, plastics, and other organic and inorganic materials.[5]

Dust preoccupies industry at every level. Fly ash—airborne bits of unburnable ash—sparks congressional hearings and requires technical measurements. (Scientists are now experimenting with a means to recover uranium from coal fly ash.) Engineers constantly seek ways to collect and dispose of dust, even enlisting robots in the effort. Production engineers endeavor to control minuscule dusts produced by mechanical friction and vibration. Computer chip manufacturers have carried the war against dust down to the level of single particles.

In the past few decades, dusts have been associated with air pollution, acid rain, and radioactive fallout. They have gone from being a local matter of factory safety to an issue of regional and even global environmental protection. Radioactive dusts awaken the most dramatic concerns. In the wake of the Chernobyl disaster, scientists across Europe sought to measure the contaminating particles spewed out by the nuclear meltdown in Ukraine.

These new dusts—though occasionally benign and even useful—have in the main become an enemy of life. Dust represents erosion, the absence of vegetation, and sterile soils. It can be taken as proof of deforestation and desertification. It can be considered evidence of destructive development.[6] Dust in its most pernicious forms is thought to threaten the biosphere itself.

Even the dimmest souls have come to recognize truth in the proposition that the smallest things can be the Achilles' heel of the greatest society. For most people today, tiny particles cast a greater shadow over this earthly garden than threats from the heavens. The infinitesimal commands attention. Be they dust particles, viruses, or errant protons, these enemies have forced us to stretch our imagination and invent technologies with which to control them. Everything this civilization values—order, pleasure, and health—requires mastery of these unseen entities.

SCIENCE ACHIEVES GREATER CONTROL OF THE SMALL

World War II accelerated the progress of science and technology into the microcosm. Scientists and technologists played tag with one another in their search for microscopic control. With mathematics and myriad theories, they defined a new microcosm. With the evolution from mechanical and electromechanical systems to electronics, miniaturization, digitalization, and software, they produced ultraprecise machines that allowed them to plumb the depths of reality.[7] With fine cutting machines and super-adhesives, they took things apart and put them together in entirely new ways.[8]

One crucial component of this revolution was the transistor, which detects and amplifies electric impulses. Transistors replaced vacuum tubes and have in turn been dramatically miniaturized and diversified by microengineering. Today millions of transistors can fit on a fingernail-sized piece of semiconductor. Computers, dependent on transistors, have become ever smaller and faster. Their defining unit, the microprocessor—an instrument originally composed of several transistors—can now comprise over a million transistors. Computers are but one demonstration of the modern ability to make goods smaller, lighter, more intricate, and more useful—and proof that power over the great is dependent on manipulation of microscopic materials and processes.

At the center of this revolution lies not simply the discovery of new materials but a newfound human ability to design and make materials, layer by layer, electron by electron. This ability, already displayed with the invention of polymers, became stunningly manifest with semiconductor materials in the 1980s when Bell Laboratories, under the direction of Frederico Capasso, developed a technique known as molecular beam epitaxy, which can "spray-paint a crystal into existence one atomic layer at a time."[9] In the world of micro-architecture, such inventions augur a new technology, carrying out a revolution, according to some, "akin to the first flaking of stone 2.5 million years ago or the primitive metallurgists who first smelted metal from rock ore 10,000 years ago" that can generate computer-designed materials to fit human desires.[10] By these lights, the periodic table—which holds the key to "every diamond, every superconductor, every three-five optoelectronic crystal, every speck of dust, every biological tissue, every material that ever was, is or will be"—is like a piano here for us to play.[11]

At the beginning of the century, atomic theory and the mastery of electricity constructed pathways into the atomic and subatomic depths. Telegraph, telephone, and radio offered evidence of the ability to command invisible currents. No sooner were X rays discovered than they were perceived as a means to penetrate the human body. (During World War I, Marie Curie used X rays on French soldiers to locate embedded shrapnel fragments.) PET scanning, ultrasound, magnetic resonance imaging, and other noninvasive diagnostic and treatment techniques have opened the door wider. Doctors now commonly diagnose and cure with machines that see what no human eye can.

Seeking to penetrate the secrets of matter and energy, scientists and technologists made the invisible their subject. They explored the entire electromagnetic spectrum.[12] Radiation studies led specifically to the discovery and application of microwaves. Useful not just for cooking, microwaves—generated by an electronic wave amplifier and accelerator—are essential to radar, long-distance telephone communication, broadcast and cable television, and radiotherapy apparatus.[13] Particle radiation—the alpha and beta rays in radioactivity and other kinds of rays from atomic and subatomic particles—is integral to the use of radiotherapy, photoelectric cells, and electronic eyes.

Contemporary scientists have supplemented their eyesight with machines that receive, measure, and record waves and pulses far too fast and fine for the human eye to detect. Of course, science had already begun to capture and control light in the nineteenth century. Cameras were used to capture images the human eye could not record; radiometers were used to detect and measure radiation; and light meters, called interferometers, used light waves to measure both interstellar distances and things as small as a half of a light wave—the limit of measurement with visible light.[14]

Twentieth-century science and technology probed much deeper into the depths of the microcosm. New particle microscopes threw a far better light on experimental subjects than Leeuwenhoek's best lenses. The traditional microscope magnified objects by up to two thousand times; the electron microscope, using a moving beam of electrons, can magnify an object approximately a million times. Using magnetic "lenses" to deflect electrons in the same way that glass lenses bend light rays, one type of electron microscope passes electrons through an object, while another bounces them off the object to create an image of it.[15] The scanning tunneling microscope (STM), invented in 1981, creates "a miniature topographic map of the hills and valleys of arrays of atoms."[16] Atomic force microscopes, invented in 1985, use electrons from the tip of a splinter of a diamond to explore the surface of individual atoms.[17] Most recently, the positron microscope, created in 1987 at the University of Michigan, uses isotopes such as sodium-22 to measure yet more finely the world of atoms. At accelerating rates, the microcosm has been breached, observed, and controlled. Our theory and machines have taken hold of what our eyes cannot directly see or our hands touch.

As physics defined one portion of the microcosm, biology provided a new lexicon of small living things. To take perhaps the most important case of all, the 1953 discovery of the structure of DNA (deoxyribonucleic acid) proved an essential step in learning how genes replicate themselves.[18] The resulting growth of molecular genetics made it possible to examine the genes in the chromosomes of different species and describe a genome (the complete set of genetic material in an individual), which opens the door to cloning animals and humans. Dolly, a sheep cloned from a six-year-old ewe to create a genetically identical lamb, was welcomed into the world on February 24, 1997. Dolly occasioned a giant hubbub in which experts and laypeople were invited to debate the consequences of human manipulation of nature's most hidden, intimate, and tiny parts.[19]

Cloning, which can be understood as the essence of miniaturization and manipulation of life, challenges our values and stimulates our imaginations as little else. In one sense, cloning, defined as the asexual reproduction of the nucleus of a cell from the body of a single parent,

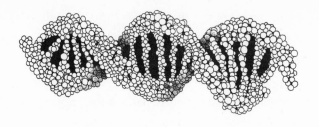

DNA

is as old as horticultural cutting and grafting, or, in nature, the asexual reproduction of organisms such as bacteria. In the contemporary sense, it connotes replication by genetic manipulation. In this sense, the cloning of Dolly, which captured the world's attention, surpassed all previous forms of cloning, which were predicated on the use of chromosomes from embryos or juveniles rather than from adult organisms. Dolly was generated from a specialized adult cell, making her an exact genetic copy—a clone—of her mother.[20]

The cloning of Dolly raises the question of whether human control over the invisible will lead to genetic self-engineering. The ongoing Human Genome Project, a major scientific effort to map all the genes on every human chromosome, opens up the possibility, albeit still remote, of humans shopping for their own kind. At the end of this fifteen-year project—which unlike most large endeavors is proceeding well ahead of schedule—for better or worse, the blueprint of human life itself will be visible to humanity. Science can now command what a few decades ago people could not even imagine.[21]

Today the manipulation of the living and nonliving small proceeds at a staggering rate. Human imagination is dragged into tangled and perplexing microuniverses. Once upon a time royalty amused itself by harnessing fleas to miniature cannons. Now bacteria—millions and millions of which could ride bareback on the smallest flea—serve more utilitarian purposes. They not only continue their age-old tasks of fermenting beer and wine, but they are also used to produce pharmaceuticals and optic fibers. The first microbes patented in the United States (in 1972) gobble up oil spills around the world. Today bacteria clean up cyanide in streams and make enzymes for snipping DNA, a first step in genetic engineering. An American bug bank keeps a stock of 55,000 frozen cell cultures for future work.[22]

Medicine has been part of this redefinition of the small. Utilizing ever subtler techniques, instruments, and laboratories, it has entered into even more intimate relationships with the details of human life. Allergists have entered the bedroom and pointed an accusing finger not at mites (the tiniest of known spiders) but at their wastes as the most insidious causes of allergies and asthma.

Medicine inventories people's environments. It counts the finest pollens (*pollen* means dust in Latin), showing that ten thousand pollen grains could fit on the head of a pin. (Certain pollens are so "tiny and uniform they have been used to calibrate instruments that measure in the thousandths of an inch.")[23] Pharmacologists' subtlest creations—which still involve such timeless tools as pestle and mortar and such perennial acts as crushing and mixing—have gone right to people's minds, altering their moods, pleasures, and lives. Ground into minute particles, lithium—the lightest known metal, also used in thermonuclear bombs, ceramics, and optical glass—was first widely prescribed for manic-depressive illness in the early 1970s. Now it helps hundreds of thousands of people live normal lives (though not without side effects). Prozac, commonly administered as a powder in a capsule, emerged in the 1990s as an immensely popular and controversial drug for the treatment of depression. Pills create a four-way conversation among drug, patient, doctor, and society. The conversation centers on what the finest grains imaginable can do to ease the suffering of mind and body, and at what cost.

Other sciences also consider minuscule things. Geologists measure mountains and seas by the accumulation of sediments of the finest clays. Paleontologists scan the micrographs of four conodonts—which may have been the closest living invertebrate relative of vertebrates— mounted on a pinhead in a debate over the origins of that species and of human life itself.[24] Palynologists—pollen experts—use the nearly indestructible shells of pollen to determine continental drift, the advance and retreat of ice ages, the formation of seas, and the rise and fall of mountains.[25] Prehistoric termites trapped in amber yield DNA twenty-five million years old.[26]

In Germany, radioastronomers take the search for the small to the universe at large. They scan space for molecules that might indicate the origins of life. The Cologne radiotelescope they use "is so sensitive that it could register the spectral lines of a candle burning on the moon." More impressive, it identifies spectral lines from "photons that become dark clouds near the heart of the Milky Way 25,000 light-years away." While they have not yet confirmed the theoretical assumption that 90 percent of the total mass of the universe is located in invisible space between visible galaxies—the great hidden dust of things—a

Termite in amber

German radioastronomer associated with the project waxed poetic in 1992 when he concluded that "in all probability the atoms and molecules of the whole of mankind have passed through other stars more than once."[27] On the basis of X-ray pictures of three galaxies 150 million light-years away and as massive as 500 billion suns, the Roentgen satellite confirmed that 99 percent of the universe is invisible and suggests that 90 percent of it may consist of particles never seen on earth.[28]

The computer adds profoundly—as does our age's overall concern for calculation and statistics—to recognition of the presence of small and invisible things. With an immense number of single switches (set to be either 0 or 1), computers carry out intricate functions to chart the path of a spaceship, plumb the unseen depths of the earth, or design the wings of a plane. The more powerful the machine, the smaller its parts. Or perhaps it is the other way around: the smaller its parts, the more powerful the machine. In this world of computers, intricacy means nearly everything.

Practicing molecular engineering and offering the dream of atomic engineering, nanotechnology encompasses several sciences, including chemistry, physics, electrical engineering, and materials science. Its practitioners work in dimensions smaller than the wavelength of light (100 nanometers, or 10^{-9} meter), inspecting viruses (10 nm) and DNA (2–3 nm). Some of the materials they work with can survive for only a trillionth of a second. One impetus for their work is contemporary chemistry, which adds half a million new compounds each year to an estimated twelve million specific molecular compounds.[29] Fueling their imagination is the work of molecular scientists, who, building from the bottom up, have produced such novel materials as nylon, Tyvek, Teflon, and superglue, and micromachinists, who, "after creating the first transistor in 1948, learned to build logic and computation machines with micron-scale components, thereby generating a global industry second only to agriculture."[30]

These scientists' work lends weight to Alfred North Whitehead's assertion: "The reason we are on a higher imaginative level is not because we have finer imagination, but because we have better instruments."[31] Their achievements—like so much of contemporary science—depend on a greatly enhanced ability to measure things. After barely twenty years of existence, atomic and molecular detectors and sensors operate much of our world, alerting us to smoke, identifying drunk drivers, opening and closing doors, and reading and copying our writings and markings. The finest of these machines also give scientists the ability to combine spatial resolution with tunneling microscopy and the time resolution of ultrafast optics. Together they yield a powerful tool for the investigation of dynamic atomic phenomena, allowing the close tracking of molecular reactions. Although reliable engineering and manufacturing techniques have yet to be developed, these innovations point the way to new orders of materials with unique physical properties.[32]

Richard Feynman—whose visionary 1959 lecture "There's Plenty of Room at the Bottom" opened a door to nanotechnology—speculated that the possibility of "arranging atoms one by one the way we want them" would create the potential for atomic-scale assembly of machines and ultraminiaturized computers.[33] Nanotechnology has evolved to encompass not only computational devices but also tiny mechanical devices equipped with micron-sized bearings, gears, cams, and clutches. Among enthusiasts' projections are immunity machines that "could destroy viruses roaming the bloodstream. Inside these robots would reside tiny gears no bigger than a protein molecule."[34]

Ultrafine technology means ultrafine measurement (see table 1 for examples). Beams of light replaced lines on dense alloys to define standard measures. From 1945 to 1950, adding further precision to light measurements, the U.S. Bureau of Standards developed improved length standards using light from mercury-198, an isotope formed by transmuting atoms of gold in nuclear reactors.[35] Precision has increasingly depended on radiation.[36]

Even in the late twentieth century, most people are ignorant of science's finest units of measure. Everyone in the West, however, lives amid the products and processes that these fine measures make possible. Automobiles, appliances, and workplace machinery run on computer chips and are manufactured to more and more precise tolerances. Households have sensors and automatic devices of all sorts to regulate heat and humidity, to turn lights on and off, to supply water, to run

TABLE I.
MEASURES OF THE MICROCOSM

Description	Length (meters)
1 meter (m)	1
length, cat	7×10^{-1}
1 centimeter (cm)	10^{-2}
length, small insect	7×10^{-3}
1 millimeter (mm)	10^{-3}
diameter, human hair	8×10^{-5}
lower limit of vision, unaided human eye	4×10^{-5}
red blood cell	7×10^{-6}
chromosome	10^{-6}
1 micron (ṃ)	10^{-6}
small bacterium	2×10^{-7}
virus	10^{-8}
1 nanometer (nm)	10^{-9}
diameter, atoms	$1-2 \times 10^{-10}$
1 angstrom (Å)	10^{-10}
1 picometer	10^{-12}
diameter, atomic nucleus	10^{-14}
1 femtometer	10^{-15}

Adapted from Herbert Klein, *The Science of Measurement: A Historical Survey* (New York: Dover Publications, 1974), 191–92.

sump pumps, to operate timers, to warn of fires, and to detect radon. In the near future, houses will function by remote control using a computer linked to the telephone and television. Control, increasingly hidden below and within, will become ever less visible, ever more commanding.

Peoples of the developed world have willingly delivered themselves into the hands of the manufactured unseen. Our dependence has been the consequence of a succession of revolutions. The agricultural, urban, and industrial revolutions were the first; the electric and now the electronic revolution have driven us on. The amount of time between successive revolutions has declined dramatically, and our reliance on unseen things has grown proportionally. The buttons on our radios and televisions, the timers on our stoves and furnaces, our children's allergy shots—these things and more make command of the small a common presumption. More and more, our surroundings are invisibly administered and illuminated to our taste.

This desire to organize, regulate, and manipulate the minute and unseen has already spread to the rest of the world. Russian president Boris Yeltsin first consulted with America's most prominent heart surgeon before undergoing a coronary bypass. Saintly Mother Teresa of India received the most sophisticated medical care possible. Control of our world, especially when it comes to well-being, is an emulated Western good, and more than anything else accounts for Western material and perceived cultural superiority.

CHAPTER EIGHT

THE SNAKE STILL LURKS

> The planet is nothing but a crazy quilt of micro soups scattered all over its 196,938,800-square-mile surface. We, as individuals, can't see them, or sense their presence in any useful manner. The most sophisticated of their species have the ability to outwit or manipulate the one microbial sensing system *Homo sapiens* possess: our immune system.　　　　　—Laurie Garrett, *The Coming Plague*

> In the 1990s, we can see that for each disease conquered, another has emerged or reemerged. Scores of infections have shattered the dream of a sanitary utopia.
> 　　　　　—Arno Karlen, *Man and Microbes*

However Edenic the human environment—however dust-free, illuminated, and exactly calibrated it has become—the serpent has not been expelled from it. He still has legions of tiny allies, though these cannot be, as they once were, wrapped up in a package called Misery and Fate and accepted as life's unalterable conditions. These fresh enemies are unique. Each has its own name and a capacity to cause its own kind of fear and dread. Medusa-headed cancer, for example, metastasizes differently in each person's imagination. (One person sees the sun's ultraviolet rays piercing the ozone layer and corrupting skin cells. Another sees his uncle dying of lung cancer.) Poisons that are suspected to lurk in air, water, and food strike terror in the hearts of many. Visions of cholesterol, accumulating on artery walls and breaking loose like ice floes in a river until it dams up the heart, make the counting of calories an ominous self-audit of the accreting death from within.

Society now carefully weighs little things. Incrementally, cryptically, the small and invisible can hurt and kill. They threaten at the table, in the basement, in the bedroom, and at the water tap. Danger lurks wherever knowledge and imagination can reach. Fears of drugs, poisons, viruses, radiation, and hundreds of chemicals accumulate in contemporary people. We are not at home in the garden of our own making.

Among the many new enemies are dusts. Complex and multifarious, they attack the earth. In 1962, Rachel Carson called attention to a new order of dreadful dusts in *Silent Spring*. She described the deadly effect of pesticides like DDT on the natural environment. Promising to free crops from dreaded insects, these pesticides had poisoned the food chain, from the smallest bacteria to the largest mammals.

While the masses packed the moviehouses to entertain themselves with fabricated fears of bug-laden asteroids and extraterrestrial alien spores, Carson enumerated truly lethal earthly enemies. Approximately two hundred insecticides and herbicides were produced in the United States, and another five hundred were annually finding their way to U.S. markets. Cumulatively, they were destroying the foundation of life itself, Carson charged. Drawing a parallel between them and nuclear contamination—particularly from strontium-90, which had recently been discovered to collect in the milk of cows and human mothers—Carson argued that pesticides were accumulating at significant rates in animal and plant tissue. They penetrated cells and "shattered or altered the very material of heredity upon which the shape of the future depends."[1]

Delivered in liquid and dry forms, these invisible killers collected wherever they were nonselectively applied. "In less than two decades," Carson wrote, "they have been thoroughly distributed throughout the world and they occur virtually everywhere. . . . They have been found in fish in remote lakes, in earthworms burrowing in the soil, in the eggs of birds—and in man himself." They have "immense power not merely to poison but to enter into the most vital processes of the body and change them in sinister and deadly ways."[2] They can destroy enzymes, block the process by which the body receives its energy, prevent organs from functioning, cause cancer, and precipitate genetic mutations.

Carson, whose work rested on an emerging ecological science, told the story of these hidden lethal processes with powerful images from around the world of scorched lands, sterilized waters, and animals dying in swarms. She quoted René Dubos—they "creep on [men] unobtrusively"—to describe these invisible enemies. In "the ecology of the world within our bodies," she wrote, "minute causes produce mighty effects . . . a change at one point, in a single molecule even, may reverberate throughout the entire system to initiate changes in seemingly unrelated organs and tissues."[3] These changes may destroy the cells "as a chemical factory," denying the body the very oxygen it needs to live.

Carson pointed out that many of these chemicals are mutagens: they alter chromosomes and cells. They carry the potential to turn the living into monsters. For Carson, the serpent was a human creation, not a fallen angel: the science that had brought many unseen pathogenic organisms under control had also created, at the molecular level, a carcinogenic society.[4]

Carson's apocalyptic vision portrays the nemesis of the minute as a response to human conquest of the small. The hubris of command invites catastrophe. Carson noted that across the globe thousands of beneficial insects were being destroyed by pesticides while deadlier, chemical-resistant pests emerged. The fate of chemical society, in which humanity had placed such hope, would turn on its most perverse and errant molecules, and so those who lived by poison would perish by poison.

AN ECOLOGICAL VISION OF THE MICROCOSM

Carson's role was to define the ethical and the metaphorical parameters of an ecological vision of the earth. She preached the need for humans to live in harmony with the tiniest parts of the natural order. Nature, as she understood it, could no longer be conceived of as observable to humans. Rather, much of what was most important about nature was hidden from sight. Nothing was too petite to be part of Carson's zoo; no link between the organic and inorganic was too subtle or cryptic to be explored.

This ecological view pushes human imagination to care about everything on the planet. An awe of life not dissimilar to the Hindu reverence for all living things is its emotional kernel. In this view, all things have a place in the eternal flux; everything depends on everything else; the star shines in the smallest ripple of water.

Carson's ecology constituted a fresh perception of the small and the invisible, which took form and became popular in the 1970s and 1980s. It was chillingly justified by events, foremost among them the Vietnam War. The war formed a stage on which the world's strongest industrial, nuclear, and chemical power, the United States, acted out the part of a sinister poisoner of nature. The country's use of antipersonnel weapons and defoliants made it, along with its chemical-based industries, appear an enemy of life right down to the level of cell and molecule.

Other events reinforced the developing ecological view and its understanding of the unseen. In the late 1960s, at Dugway Proving Ground in Utah, the U.S. Army accidentally killed several thousand sheep with nerve gas. Many who read of the event, no matter how great their outrage, sensed that the powers of the era had transformed them, too, into innocent lambs being led to slaughter by the state. News of the poison gas—the most sinister and concealed element of the arms race—awakened memories of World War I and the Nazi gassing of the Jews, and it exacerbated current fears that technological civilization would poison everything. The public's dread of nerve gas has been kept alive by the revelations of disarmament negotiations, chemical accidents like the 1984 disaster in Bhopal, India, the Soviet use of poisonous gases in Afghanistan, and the terrorist use of poison gases in the Tokyo subway.

Other events of the past three decades have driven the human imagination microscopically inward and downward. Oil spills have produced regular accusations that contemporary society is poisoning the earth, drop by black drop. Single acts of pollution have been taken to be revelatory of self-poisoning. Groundwater has been declared contaminated, rivers polluted, lakes acidified, and seas atrophied. Animals of all sizes and types—from whales to whooping cranes—have been declared endangered. Whole regions—forests, deserts, prairies, and wetlands—have been pronounced dead or in danger of extinction. Revelations of toxic and nuclear waste dumps have created powerful images of a nation covered with wounds from which rivers of lethal, invisible chemicals ooze.

As water and soil pollution invisibly menaced from below, air pollution menaced from above. In 1858 London experienced what became known as the Great Stink. So much sewage flowed into the Thames that Parliament ground to a halt because of the stench. The incident helped precipitate a national cleanup. In 1952 four thousand deaths were attributed to London's "pea-soup" fog.[5] But only in the late 1960s and 1970s did air pollution—known as smog—become a globally recognized menace. Smog alerts warned people with allergies and asthma to stay indoors, and children were forbidden to go outside to play.

Responding to the emerging crisis, scientists plunged ahead in their study of aerosols, which are essentially atmospheric dusts.[6] They identified a range of chemical particles and a complex set of chemical reactions that contributed to pollution of the atmosphere. Aerosols range in size from coarse natural particles emitted by volcanoes and sea plants to fine synthetic particles created by high-temperature combustion.[7] Many of these unseen particles react chemically to form legions of invisible enemies, harming sensitive ecosystems.[8]

Public concern about soil, water, and air pollution led to government regulation of industrial emissions. Capturing, filtering, and testing for particulates became occupational specialties. Pollution control became a skill and engendered a federal agency as well as many state agencies.

In 1978 the U.S. government banned aerosol spray cans containing chlorofluorocarbons (CFCs), which were understood to destroy the ozone layer that protects life on earth from the sun's ultraviolet rays. (From 1973 to 1985 the number of skin cancer deaths increased by 26 percent.)[9] The popular imagination was stretched when people were told that a squirt of a morning deodorant or hairspray could damage the atmosphere and that carbon dioxide emissions form a layer of particles that traps heat in the atmosphere, causing global warming, which, in turn, could cause global flooding from the melting of the polar ice caps. But people were also asked to consider the opposite possibility: that industrial and agricultural emissions might form a screen—as volcanic dusts have in the past—that would block out sunlight, thus cooling the atmosphere and causing a new ice age. Only the most obtuse missed the main message: humans risked so distorting the natural order that they were sentencing themselves to be destroyed by frost or furnace.

Spurred by the fear of environmental degradation, new academic disciplines and government agencies sprang up in the United States.[10] In 1963 the U.S. Congress passed the Clean Air Act. In 1970 the government formed the Environmental Protection Agency. The first version of the Clean Water Act passed Congress in 1972. Europe followed suit. Having long ago turned its rivers into polluted canals, eliminated most of its wildlife, and surrendered to the automobile, Europe, led by its youth, enthusiastically formed Green parties, whose popularity crested in the 1980s. The West agreed: little things are big things.

The ecological view was shared by ecologists, environmentalists, animal rights proponents, alternative energy adherents, and population-control advocates. Not without ideological and emotional similarities to earlier traditionalists who sought to defend "authentic" peasant ways against the artificial ways of the city, this novel breed of ecologists (coming almost uniformly from the educated middle and upper classes) shared a terrifying vision of microscopic life on Earth. Nature had insufficient capacity to digest all our wastes. Artificial human pollutants outstripped nature's own solvents and cleaners. In a stunning reversal of the Western view of the small, insects, worms, and bacteria were seen as nature's last defenders. They alone, it seemed, could dispose of the toxic detritus of human society.

A NEW GRID ON THE UNSEEN

The ecological view of the small superimposed itself on germ theory, just as germ theory had superimposed itself on the theory of vapors. Postulating the fundamental significance of molecular processes and microorganisms, together ecology and germ theory gave rise to an epidemiological surveillance that extended across the whole sphere of organic matter.

In contrast to germ theory, however, the ecological view equated the natural with the good. Those raised on germ theory complained that these new-wave ecologists courted a return to filth, disease, and germs. Beneficiaries of national public health regimens, and a generation or two removed from experience with epidemics of killing diseases, many of the younger adherents of what came loosely to be called the ecology movement rejected the personal health disciplines on which they had been raised. They condemned pesticides. The extreme among them turned up their noses at synthetic cleansers, and, heedless to the noses of others, they spurned artificial deodorants and soaps. They flushed their toilets less frequently to save water. They acted—often both naively and ostentatiously—as if they were immune to the diseases the preceding generation had so profoundly struggled against. Parades of dirty and accusatorial youth marched righteously under the banner of getting back to nature. They let things creep and crawl about them and welcomed dirt and dust. Oblivious to the diseases of earlier years, they judged unseen nature to be innocent.

Independent of the extreme practices and ideas of its most zealous adherents, the ecological view rested on a profound reordering of the microcosm. Redefining contamination, it produced new taboos. It determined what was polluted and not polluted in a new way. Its first demarcation was between the organic and inorganic, the natural and the synthetic, the pure and the artificial. If a product was "natural," it not only was healthy for the body but also put the user spiritually in tune with the ecosphere.

The most fervent beliefs in the ecological view produced devout observances in everyday life. As sin, however slight and subtle, separates believers from their god, so acts of polluting, however small, were understood to separate people from the cosmic order, which joins each living creature to every other living creature—ant and elephant, flower and manure pile. Like a fertile religion, the ecological view spawned many sects and followers. Its monks withdrew to the mountains and ate berries and honey. A vast number of faithful suburban middle-class believers adopted organic diets, drove their small cars less frequently, and talked about invisible, omnipresent carcinogens the way peasants once talked about the weather. They earnestly sought a natural, pure life.

The core of this faith was purity, and it required a meticulous concern for small things. Like all great belief systems, it allowed believers to classify the smallest things of everyday life while offering a sense of cosmic companionship with others (in this case, all living things). While calling for reform, it offered the ecstatic view that the details of life are a perfect miniature cosmos worthy of adulation. This view squared well with the vague pacifism of the younger generation in the United States and Europe while clashing sharply with the beliefs of an older generation proud of the battles it had fought against seen and unseen threats to the nation's well-being.

Of course, the ecological sensibility did not escape a fundamental paradox: though humans should care for nature, nature does not always care about them.

THE SNAKE RESURFACES

The demarcations of the small and the invisible made by the ecologists of the 1960s and 1970s blended with concerns about radioactive contamination. Radioactivity kept people mindful of invisible threats. As always, events instructed imagination. The 1979 accident at Three Mile Island, rife with threats of nuclear catastrophe, sounded the death knell for the expansion of nuclear energy in the United States. The actual meltdown at Chernobyl in 1988 spewed radioactivity over much of eastern and northern Europe, sparking a universal call for further study of the effects of radiation on human cells.[11] The first phases of Soviet and American disarmament, in tandem with the emergence of nuclear programs in Iraq and North Korea, raised questions about the most lethal black market of all: nuclear materials. International protests against the resumption of nuclear testing by the French in the Pacific demonstrated the vitality of public fears of subatomic particles.

Antennae for the invisible have grown on nearly every head as almost everything we eat, drink, and breathe has been judged carcinogenic. Science courts have sprung up across the nation to settle debates about the disposal of radioactive dusts and other toxic materials. Health education has taught people that exposure to even the most minuscule quantities of certain toxins can kill human beings by the millions. Having learned to measure its well-being in milligrams of food and medicine, the whole population—especially the middle classes—has adopted a new lexicon of millesimal hopes and fears.

As safe as contemporary urban dwellers are—especially when their lives are contrasted with those of their dusty peasant ancestors—they still feel menaced by minuscule enemies. As each generation removes one layer of worries, it discovers another. Today the media and governments caution the vulnerable public about chemical products, microwave ovens, and allergens. Nutritionists remind consumers that foods are poisoning them gram by gram. The old, visible enemies—like dust and worms—have been replaced by stealthier enemies. Whole buildings have been judged "sick" because of asbestos in the walls or other synthetic materials that poison the occupants. A newspaper banner exposes "The Toxic Workplace." A magazine article declares that "microbes live and breed in HVAC [heating, ventilation, and air conditioning] ducts."[12] "Sick building syndrome" has become common

1990s parlance—and workers fear that they are being poisoned daily by their computers, cell phones, chairs, and carpets.

Indeed, since the 1960s, hordes of invisible enemies have gathered on the horizon. Masses of people who have benefited more than anyone in the past from human control of the small have joined ecologists in rejecting civilization's conquest of nature. Arguments long made against Western materialism, capitalism, and imperialism have been steadily incorporated into the rhetoric of environmentalists and ecologists. Given the era's escalating and fashionable moralizing against all things Western, it is a short and chic step from indicting Western society as the exploiter of native peoples to condemning it as the violator of the biosphere.

This view of human beings' relationship with nature has undergone another twist in the past decade. The small is understood to be striking back. In *The Coming Plague,* Laurie Garrett tantalizingly suggests that the reappearance of the plague is the nemesis of progress's intrusion into the microcosm.[13] As human populations grow and interact, viruses and bacteria lose their natural hosts and make use of available human beings. The hunter becomes the hunted.

Microorganisms whose eradication was predicted by health organizations have adapted and survived. Killer diseases of yesteryear, resistant to the drugs that once controlled them, are making a frightening comeback. Syphilis, malaria, and measles once again strike people with terror.[14] Lyme disease and Rocky Mountain spotted fever are on the increase. Yellow fever and tuberculosis have reappeared in the United States. Even cases of bubonic plague have been reported in Vietnam and the United States. Tougher strains of disease have forced medicine to assemble a fresh generation of drugs. Nations worry that civilization is being beaten on the invisible battlefield of disease, where half a century ago it stood as the victor.

New diseases add new fears. In the mid-1990s, Britain was rocked by the revelation that a form of Creutzfeldt-Jakob disease, a rare and fatal brain disease, could apparently be contracted by eating meat from cows infected with bovine spongiform encephalopathy (BSE, or mad cow disease). BSE, in turn, was seemingly spread by the use of cattle feed containing the offal of sheep with scrapie, a disease that was believed not to affect other animals. When the link between Creutzfeldt-Jakob and BSE was acknowledged, more than a million cows were slaughtered and incinerated in Britain, and the British beef market collapsed. The cause of this group of diseases is believed to be a prion, a life form even smaller and more enigmatic than viruses—and one unaffected by conventional sterilization techniques.[15] Another intimidating micro-entity lurks in the garden.

In *Man and Microbes*, Arno Karlen offers a list of approximately thirty new diseases that have appeared since 1951.[16] In recent years in the United States, toxic shock syndrome, swine flu, and Legionnaires' disease have captured public attention. Even more terrifying, the vicious African hemorrhagic fevers, Lassa, Marburg, and Ebola, have appeared in the West.[17] The smallest living creatures can undo the greatest.

Though not as easily spread or instantly lethal as the new hemorrhagic diseases, the human immunodeficiency virus has killed millions and infected millions more around the world. Invisible in its nature, manifest in its consequences, it has caused passionate moral debate. But

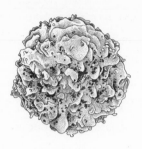

Human immunodeficiency viruses using a human white blood cell as breeding ground. Dots are budding viruses.

the truly insidious character of HIV lies in the microscopic tricks it plays on the human immune system. Constantly changing its disguises, the virus stealthily enters the white blood cells whose function is to encircle and kill trespassers. Having crippled the white cells, it leaves its host fair game for all opportunistic diseases. More than any other disease, HIV has compelled Western imagination to reopen itself to the lethal powers of the microcosm. It has proved to be the most stealthy of serpents in the garden of this generation's intimate pleasures.

Imagination (rarely a pure or keen instrument, and frequently rigidly fixed by custom or fashion) struggles to focus its metaphors and science on the newly perceived nemesis. Life is threatened from below and beyond by invisible enemies crueler than Lucretius's indifferent atoms. We have no choice but to continue to trust science and technology to control unseen entities, for the sweet garden, earth, is not yet secure.

WHO WILL TREMBLE
AT THESE MARVELS?

> Small numbers count. A small imbalance in the particle-antiparticle ratio of the early universe, for example, leads to a cosmos of 50 billion galaxies and a habitable planet Earth. A small change in cholesterol content can produce disproportionately large changes in cell functioning. The flapping of a butterfly's wing in South Asia may alter the ensuing weather over San Francisco.
> —David Toolan, "Praying in a Post-Einsteinian Universe"

> Imagination. It is the dominant faculty, master of error and falsehood, all the more deceptive for being invariably so.
> —Blaise Pascal, *Pensées*

This century's dramatic encounter with the small and the invisible portends a significant cultural revolution. "For who," in the words of Pascal, "will not marvel that our body, a moment ago imperceptible in the universe, itself imperceptible in the bosom of the whole, should now be a colossus, a world, or rather a whole compared to the nothingness beyond our reach?" Who, knowing himself to exist between "these two abysses of infinity and nothingness, will not tremble at these marvels?"[1]

The nineteenth century was about colossal things: large visions, immense undertakings, and sublime buildings. It founded profitable industries, laid tracks across continents, and opened vast acres of dust, dirt, and sand to the winds. Its urban works transformed the country- side and turned peasants into national citizens. The twentieth century, though it inherited the nineteenth century's commitment to large-scale projects, turned its attention to ultrafine and microcosmic things. It has not shuddered in awe before Pascal's second infinity of nothings. It has treated the amplitudes of the minute as a wilderness to explore and subjugate. It has dwarfed old kingdoms of the small with new worlds of the invisible. It has directed the human eye downward.

Nothing has been too small or remote for twentieth-century science to scrutinize. No sooner had atom and molecule, cell and microbe been defined than they were made gateways into countless other miniature worlds. As if they were pulling apart an endless set of Russian dolls within dolls, twentieth-century science and technology kept locating infinities within the finitude. Their findings reproduced at rates faster than ethics, politics, and common sense could comprehend. There seemed to be no bottom to things. Those who peer down continue to experience vertigo.

The twentieth century has reversed the dominant hierarchy of being. Contradicting what had been assumed since classical times—that being and form emanate downward from on high—it has argued that the microcosm is the source and explanation of the macrocosm. The truth of the great is found in the small.

At the start of this century, the astronomer's model of the galaxy— planets circling the sun—furnished a model for the atom: electrons twirling around a nucleus. Now, at century's end, the physics of the heavens has been reduced to the science of particles. Tiny things have become intriguing, and the small keeps getting smaller. Atoms have been found to contain particles and forces, which, without mass, move in pulses and waves.

Earth, heavens, and seas have been explored. Animal and plant life are scrutinized in detail.[2] The human body (a principal territory for the expansion of inquiry into the small and the unseen) has become whole continents worthy of many sciences. The manipulation of select molecules forms the basis of entire industries.

As science and technology have penetrated inward and downward, plain old dust, though still profoundly present in life—especially rural life—has lost its role as the first definition of the small. Dust is no longer presumed to constitute the surface of things. Smooth, often colorful, and water-resistant synthetic surfaces make up our roads, walls, floors, and furniture covers. Asphalt and cement (admittedly dusty to extract and make) have replaced dirt, sand, and gravel roads. Bright lawns and gardens have replaced dusty yards and open spaces.

Dust no longer constitutes a boundary between the visible and the invisible. Penetrated by tiny instruments and countless theories of the microcosm, dust has become porous. Like other barriers to light and knowledge, including skin and darkness, dust has been taken down. Its powers, real and magical, have vanished, much as ogres, angels, witches, and other invisible creatures have been pushed to the edges of experience. A target of laboratory analysis on the one hand, and of cleaners of all sorts on the other, dust has lost its ancient and metaphorical powers. It no longer declares the passage of time and the mortality of all living things; it does not conceal within itself the magic stuff of spontaneous generation; nor does it instantly transform what it settles on. The phrase "ashes to ashes and dust to dust" has lost much of its resonance, even if its truth still stands.

BEYOND DUST

The achievements of the twentieth century bring us to the question of how people in the future will experience the small and imagine the invisible. Having largely lost contact with the traditional order of the small and the invisible, how will contemporary people think and express themselves about new orders of the minuscule? What will be their relationship to microworlds not even hypothesized today?

In the last century and a half, urban industrial society has lost contact with an entire range of microscopic things that once defined the human environment and the prevailing sense of what was small. Human lives are shaped and regulated by abstract laws and distant agencies. As goods are mass manufactured, most Western people are removed from intimate work with materials. Except when engaged in hobbies or crafts, they work less and less with the fine objects and processes associated with sewing, pottery, woodworking, and even agriculture. The world our ancestors once knew in its particularities and details arrives in homogenized wholes.

Society has undergone a great cleanup. Once a given of everyday existence, dust and its allies are now considered blemishes on the good life, and gestures associated with their presence (scratching, spitting, nose picking) are judged rude. In today's world, only clean and refined things are welcome. Intrusive small things—like pimples and smelly feet, flies and mites, weeds and even pesticide molecules—have become matters for specialized treatment.

Of course, some rebels reject the sanitized world created by the great cleanup. With dirty clothes, shaggy hair, and cabins in the woods, they keep their distance from clean and orderly middle-class urban life. They wish to be pure by embracing dust and dirt, not artifice. Ever since the creation of a Bohemia in nineteenth-century Paris, a certain number of intellectuals and artists have embraced dirt and dust to taunt the bourgeoisie and affirm their ties to the earth and its uncorrupted peasantry. In some circles, usually identified with the political left, such attachments have provided an identity and justified an ideology. The artists' glorification of the basic—that which is dark, dirty, earthy, and hence fundamental, enduring, and passionate—can be seen in the paintings of Millet and Van Gogh, especially the thickly brushed and heavily trowelled paintings of the latter. Naturalists like Zola, with an eye for the harsh and the sordid, voiced the same longing in a different medium.

Artists are not alone in finding community in darkness and untidiness in a world of speed, efficiency, light, and cleanliness. Even those with no intellectual or aesthetic aspirations find it "a treat to beat their feet on Mississippi Mud" from time to time. The urge might amount to a visit to a cousin's farm, a week of roughing it in the wilderness, or working up a sweat cutting firewood. For a portion of each modern generation, the dust and dirt of preceding generations vanish into an aura of nostalgia. Much of what underpins the environmental movement's defense of the natural may be a search for simplicity and community in an increasingly complex age.

As dust and dirt have been removed from the center of synthetic and regulated lives, they have become the source of quaint metaphors such as "so much dust in a dust storm," "dust bunnies," "beggar's velvet," and "slut's wool." As dust, chiggers, and all sorts of irritating vermin have lost their sting in the human environment, they have also lost their hold on language. Their places have been taken by the contemporary language of scientific discovery and technological invention. Chips, bits, and bytes, bacteria, viruses, and DNA provide the metaphors that fill everyday conversation. Insofar as people become the words and metaphors they use, are we witnessing the formation of a new mind and, thus, a new people?

The new microcosmic order bids farewell to a world of images fashioned out of things seen and touched. It undoes the language and metaphors out of which imagination once constructed a rich and sublime invisible realm and provides a new order of experience and imagination. Indeed, with bodies swaddled in new comforts and senses stimulated by an artificial world of sanitized surfaces, contemporary people no longer imagine with much vividness or elasticity the small and invisible as presented by folklore and religion. At the same time, they are preoccupied with contemporary microentities on which their comfort and survival depend. In short, contemporary people are married to a new microcosm which, though too diverse and profound to understand, is too imposing and encompassing to ignore.

NEW EXPERIENCES, NEW PEOPLES, NEW MINDS

Beginning in the late nineteenth century in Western technological society, fresh groups of people and new types of minds configured themselves around the notion that nothing in the world was too small to be cleaned up. Through the first half of this century, the great cleanup insisted not only on an orderly and dust-free environment but also on one free of germs and toxins. The underlying material basis of this unprecedented expectation was humble stuff such as water pipes, pumps, and sewer lines.

Cadres of public health crusaders, along with the institutions they conscripted into service, formed regiments intent on dominating the microscopic. Passionate, even obsessed, they denounced the presence of dust and germs in the most intimate quarters of city, family, and body.

In conjunction with the banishment of undesirable minutiae, a new aesthetic arose. With the reins of control hidden in cables and pipes below the ground, and in wires threaded through walls and gathered in communication closets, the new aesthetic was predicated on the notion that people should see only what they wished to.

The new aesthetic (from which a few hermits and many artists dissented) declared that the world need no longer be dusty and dark— not even at night! It affirmed: Let light shine forth. Let there be color everywhere. Let the world be a pleasant garden. Let every woman and child be dressed in colorful clothing, as bright as a sunlit bank of flowers. Of course, women understood, as few men did, the cost of this aesthetic. It required constant vigilance and exertion against the rebellious and intrusive small. Women, who for generations had grasped that harmony and beauty require mastery of the petite and the particular, found that their new households required knowledge of machines, medicines, and cleaning agents and the wizardry to remove spots and stains. And as if maintaining a spotless home were not difficult enough, society also now demanded artful self-beautification of face and figure. The American housewife of the 1940s and 1950s—the queen of cleaning—was equipped with goods and bullied by social pressure to master the worlds of self and home as none of her foremothers had ever been asked to do.

In this increasingly see-through world, dust and dirt stood out visibly. The call to clean grew stronger. Power over the small meant responsibility for it. What escaped this new conscience and breed of cleaners hid in the wilderness of the unperceived.

The children of these dust and germ fighters, true to their lineage, never doubted that humans could and should control the small and invisible. One branch of these children, the environmentalists, while never doubting how much human intervention had distorted the ecological order of life, held firm to the proposition that humans could live in intimate harmony with nature, even at the molecular level. A second branch—who might be called the children of light—focused passionately on eradicating all blemishes from human experience. Their hegemonic confidence has extended from the ordering of the microworld to eliminating all pain and suffering and removing every instance of corruption and prejudice in the Augean stable of politics. Truly, they belong to a civilization that has banished dust and dirt.[3] They are the ultimate heirs of the radical Enlightenment, which, acting with the full force of the Industrial Revolution behind it, would have purified the world to match its imagined perfection.[4] These children of light do not realize that the good depends more on pumps and pipes than on moral preaching.

We all confess consanguinity with these two groups in our shared belief that the small and the invisible can be known and manipulated.

Medicine, more than anything, has forged the crucial link between contemporary consciousness and the new scientific and technological microcosm with its successful diagnosis and manipulation of the unseen.[5] Medicine has provided the language and metaphors of infection, disease, and germs. It has made *X ray, angiogram, CAT scan,* and *magnetic resonance* common terms. It has made the most refined medical practices everyday parlance as they become individuals' best hope for wellness. Continually holding out new hopes for health, comfort, and longevity, medicine has simultaneously fought lethal new microenemies and called attention to the dangers lurking in everyday human acts.

In the second half of this century, environmentalism further sensitized society to the powers of the unseen. The movement warned of a long list of invisible lethal enemies, including industrial wastes, toxic pesticides, and radioactive dusts. Masters of molecular suspicion, environmentalists (not always inaccurately) hypothesized monsters hiding in all human undertakings. The appearance of resistant strains of insects, bacteria, and viruses, and the emergence of terrifying diseases such as AIDS and Ebola, have been interpreted as signs of nature's vengeance.

Public health, environmentalism, and ecology were not alone in teaching twentieth-century society about the importance of the small and the invisible. Commonplace inventions like the telephone and television offered convincing proof of the powers of the unseen. Now sensors open doors, pop up perfectly browned toast, scan foods at checkout counters, set factories in motion, and initiate and cancel space flights. They read the surfaces of atoms and design the molecules for new products. Machines have become the eyes and hands of contemporary industry, whose most innovative thinkers predict molecular machines on the basis of their "silicon dreams."[6]

Virtual reality takes civilization a step further into an artificial world. A fruit of contemporary scientific imagination, it ushers human beings into a computer-generated replica of reality. Already serving a range of human activities, computers, when perfected, portend involving all human senses in their simulations and sealing the identity of humanity and machine.

Virtual reality is in tune with a society in which children are tethered to video games, laboratories are indispensable, and computer-generated situations offer instruction for everything from flying Piper Cubs to docking space stations and fighting future smart wars. Virtual reality conforms to the expectations of a world in which (thanks to books, film, television, CDs, and computers) legions of people already have more contact with representations of life than with life itself. It fits a people who know more about computers and screens than soils and rivers. Virtual reality is the logical culmination of a society whose members' lives and minds are removed from direct contact with the stuff of the world—its dust and dirt—and are constructed around the refinement and manipulation of human and natural environments.

A supporter of virtual reality holds out the hope that in the end humanity's self-invented virtual realities will not cut us off from history, nature, and culture. Virtual reality, she optimistically argues, "may function as a link from the technological manifestations of humanity back to the world that technology has ostensibly supplanted. . . . And in doing so, it may even offer a way to imagine ourselves, technology and all, as part of the natural world."[7]

Whether human control of the microcosm will, as the worst dystopias have it, lead to humanity's enslavement to its own creations is an open question. However, the indisputable fact is that humanity, to unprecedented and accelerating degrees, depends on knowledge of the microworld and new orders of materials and entities constructed by humans. The contemporary world increasingly turns on the human discovery, making, and control of the small and the invisible. Both the sublime and the mundane are increasingly encrypted in codes, etched on chips, or deciphered from DNA. Those in contact with contemporary science and technology know that what they see and touch is a mere reflection of the microscopic and atomic reality. Truth, they recognize, is not found by gazing above but by looking below. Even if they do not know his name and care not an iota for classical philosophy or its consolations, they admit that Lucretius was correct: the world turns on atoms. But they, unlike him, insist we study and master the course of these atoms.

IMAGINING A NEW IMAGINATION

What are the consequences of the growing control of the minuscule by human imagination? Will the new microcosmic concepts, procedures, and products furnish a new set of images and metaphors that will constitute a new imagination? Will the new order lead imagination to exercise and develop itself in rich and creative ways?

Surely the tools, measures, products, and conceptions of contemporary science and technology are noticed even by the dullest imaginations. They demand conceptualizing the small and the invisible afresh. They rely on abstract mathematics. They require syntheses across many fields. Dissemination of fresh findings stimulates additional creative research. All this suggests that the new microcosm accounts for new forms of imagination and, perhaps, a new imagination itself.

The proposition has already been affirmed that the revolution of the small and the invisible has altered twentieth-century views of nature and human beings' place in it. Science and technology have established relations with vast new kingdoms beyond the boundary of dust. They have provided more than a theoretical staircase—a structured descent—into orders hidden below the senses. They have established a familiar countryside reaching out from the human eye and hand into the surrounding terrain of germs and atoms.

One no longer passes beyond dust and darkness into encounters with imaginary and fantastic creatures, as those of former ages did. The "beyond" for the medieval imagination—be it reached by a mysterious voyage, death, intoxication, or spell—was imagined as life-size. It was seen to be inhabited by the dead, saints, and other anthropomorphic and animal creatures. These beings were diminished by the extension of religious orthodoxy and political sovereignty. Their very habitat was subsequently destroyed by the transformation of the city and countryside in the nineteenth century. In this century, science and technology have further domesticated the unseen, creating their own unique gatekeepers and guides into the worlds hidden below dust and darkness.

Schools, books, commerce, and media have peopled human imagination with new entities. Bigfoot and the Loch Ness monster now make fewer and fewer appearances. UFOs and ETs—clothed in scientific wrappings—must press hard to find a place in minds captivated with the real wonders of the new microsciences and technologies. Science-fiction writers and filmmakers are driven to appeal to popular imagination with tales of genetic mutation, germ warfare, and ecological catastrophe. Even the huge monsters of Jurassic Park owe their conception to contemporary research on DNA.

With traditional invisible entities in retreat, will science's new tiny entities dominate the unknown in human imagination? Surely a kind of revolution is under way, bringing with it new images. It alters society's sense of what is lethal. It redefines bodies, gestures, and daily hygiene. It transforms—and grows out of the transformation of—human relations with dust and darkness, as well as the entire realm of the minuscule and the unseen.

This revolution gives a large part of human imagination over to scientific institutions and their experts. Ordinary people, who speak with only rudimentary knowledge of atoms, cells, and computer chips, learn to talk and pray—at least in part—in the language these experts furnish. For most people, the price of admission to this newly assembled microcosm is negligible. It amounts mainly to doing what they do anyway: purchasing new and better goods and services; showing more concern for hygiene; and making occasional visits to a doctor. Who could resist entering the tent of the new microworld, when so little effort is required to defeat pain and secure comfort?

LAST THINGS ABOUT LITTLE THINGS

Will this transformation of the human relationship to the small and the invisible (to ask our question for the last time) come to constitute a revolution in imagination? I would like to answer this question affirmatively. It would be a delight for the author of a book on such a minute subject as dust to be able to make such a large announcement as the emergence of a new imagination. Unfortunately, my answer is equivocal.

There are several reasons why I don't believe that the contemporary microcosm—and the concepts, practices, and institutions associated with it—will create unique ways of imagining. First, what is obvious but fundamental, human beings think and feel anthropomorphically. We shape our images of things to fit our body size, feelings, interests, and moral and dramatic purposes. We cannot escape making ourselves the measure of all things big and small. Our fundamental emotions and wants will not, at least over the long term, be inhibited by new and subtle sciences.

Nothing is too great or too tiny for human prayer or poetry. Human hearts and metaphors will not be bounded. David Toolan illustrates this in a recent article, "Praying in a Post-Einsteinian Universe," by anthropomorphically connecting human beings' place in the universe to the particles of the dust at the beginning of the universe:

> Indeed, our connection and belonging lie so deep that we cannot even define our identities without including . . . the whole sweep of cosmic evolution. "I am that," we can now say with the Hindu Upanishads—star dust, earth stuff, a being literally conceived in far-parts of the universe and seeded here on this planet to make a difference to the cosmos, to strike a chord. . . . It's as if all the star dust in our DNA, the microbes that swim in our cells, the humble algae that gave us breathable atmosphere—yes all of nature—were expectant, waiting on us to finish the cosmic symphony well.[8]

Second, for the sake of nothing less than life itself, human beings—as recent psychological literature suggests—close off considerable portions of reality and perceive other parts of it through rose-colored glasses.[9] Only depressed people are realistic about life's possibilities, whereas the schizophrenic are uniquely accurate in perceiving life's connections and disjunctions. Patriots do not look too closely at the real conditions and motives of their fellow citizens, any more than lovers look too closely at each other's skin. Happy people choose to see only what they wish.

In *Morality and Imagination*, Yi-Fu Tuan offers a variety of reasons why humans seldom put their great endowment of imagination to use. He considers most important the need to be efficient: "Efficiency requires that most of the time we ignore the rich texture of reality to attend to only one aspect of it—its use." Implicit in the tools human beings use are one-dimensional approaches to the world. Routine, which makes the world schematic, helps exclude much from consideration. Finally, fatigue encourages humans to reduce the world to "the landmarks and directions necessary to finding our way home."[10]

Third, the house of the human mind, capable of both incredible resistance to and compartmentalization of new ideas, also welcomes all kinds of images. However, few are welcomed beyond the threshold of sentience into the ballroom of full consciousness. The mind does not need to throw out the old to make room for the new, although once in a while it does precisely that. There are periods, especially when life and well-being are threatened, when the small and invisible cannot be ignored. Then they force themselves on the imagination, often amid a stir and conflict of thoughts, images, and feelings. Usually, however, the mind houses new and old, large and small, traditional and scientific views side by side, without the pairs ever so much as meeting, though bizarre and idiosyncratic syntheses of them do pop up in individuals and are not uncommon in the culture at large.

Fourth, moral and religious considerations both close and open the mind to the unseen. Small and invisible things can go unacknowledged because they contradict standing moral perceptions. Groups deny the microscopic findings of the day because they are evidence of the world being otherwise than their belief system represents it. Contrariwise, traditional Hindu culture predisposes people to divide almost the entire world of things, however small, into the pure and the impure and to imagine invisible souls in all living things, ordaining their birth, travail, and death as part of a great universal and eternal process of reincarnation.

Fifth, certain invisible entities survive and command elements of human imagination. Even if less prayed to and more attenuated than ever before, the dead still retain powers over the living. Their entanglement with human imagination survived the Reformation and Enlightenment. Though dramatically diminished, other elements of magic, superstition, and religion still haunt human imagination.

Within people's minds there remains a strong inclination to believe in a God—or some force—who guides all things, seen and unseen, small and mighty. A Methodist hymn revealingly runs, "Because he has his eyes on the sparrow / He cares for me." Human yearnings for order, justice, love, and mercy—happiness and pleasure too—entreat God to deflect the smallest particles or subdue the most rebellious cells. Science and technology have yet to postulate something that human beings will not pray to change—or to exploit, as the histories of radiation and electricity amply testify, in quack cures involving invisible forces.

Human beings simply do not willingly sacrifice their lives to fate, or their fates to the blind course of atoms. They insist that atoms, molecules, cells, and genes fit human tales and emotions. When it comes to getting well, or simply having one's way on something important, people adjust their prayers to what is required. They do not hesitate to ask the majestic God of the heavens to alter the course of a single cell or molecule. The drive to anthropomorphize is as deeply ingrained in human thought as the human person is rooted in the physical body, averse to death and pain, and averse to a meaning and will imposed on him other than his own.

The microcosmic orders do not serve human needs as the dead and God once did. Though awesome in intricacy, energy, and speed, the new microcosm forms no pantheon and promises no mercy, no mission, no community, no friendship. It has no set rituals, no sure priests, no ruling theology, no freeing message, and no caring creature. Powerful and particular? Yes. A worldview of sorts? Maybe. A religion? No.

The new worlds of the small and invisible do not yet even constitute a certain cosmology. The continual addition of novel and fresh elements leave them short of symmetry. One does not see a crystalline and enduring order when one peers into the stir of infinitesimal bits below. It does not even appear to have a bottom. Its masters still lack devices to measure the smallest bits and chart their vaporizing speeds. Even their knowledge is not whole. Rather, it is tentative, rigged together by complex mathematics, stray intuitions, bold hypotheses, occasionally homey metaphors, and the need for odd and tenacious observation. Indeed, the whole field of physics fell decades ago under the shadow of indeterminacy. According to Heisenberg's indeterminacy principle, if things are measured as waves, their frequencies are miscalculated; and if computed by their frequency, their wavelengths are miscalculated. And if that were not enough, light itself distorts the object observed, which paradoxically results in the idea that we cannot see what we wish to see once we cast light on it.[11]

Converts are not won to a religion or even a worldview by uncertainty and complexity. Human minds are not captivated by things that do not fit their bodily-sized metaphors, their self-dramatizing stories, their earthbound moral imaginations, or their heartfelt emotional needs. Mortal human beings—creatures of skin, bone, and dust—want to do more than contemplate the infinitude of grains of sand on a beach or calculate the quivering path of a rising fleck of dust. And so new and novel images, concepts, and practices associated with the contemporary microcosm are not fully assimilated into language. Older metaphors are still invoked to mediate, negotiate, and define what lies below and beyond human eye and hand. Anthropomorphists to the bone, human beings pound all things into a shape to fit their stories. Their conversations, interests, and imaginations remain tethered to local wells.

Armies of experts and specialists in the new microworlds relieve people of the burden of taking these worlds too seriously, of having to struggle to conceive what they cannot perceive. As they increasingly rely on doctors and medical tests to tell them how they are feeling and what is going on inside them, so they trust experts to monitor the unseen worlds that encircle their lives. Unless knowledge of the minute is needed for health or offers a chance to be rich, why should human reach exceed its grasp?

Another reason why human imagination will not be transformed by the microworlds of science and technology is that human beings have bodies. Bodies place humans in a world in which they have contact with darkness, death, and dust. They are constantly compelled to measure the small by their bodies—fingertips, lips, and eyes. These impose a scale on all things perceived. The imagination cannot wander far or long from the imposition of body size. To state this idea another way, human beings are fastened to the old order by bodies and senses, which remain the first gauges of smallness and greatness. And this is but to paraphrase Alexander Pope's reply to the microscopists in his *Essay on Man:*

> Why has not Man a microscopic eye?
> For this plain reason, Man is not a Fly.
> Say what the use, were finer optics giv'n,
> T'inspect a mite, not comprehend the heav'n?
> Or touch, if tremblingly alive all o'er,
> To smart and agonize at every pore?
> Or quick effluvia darting thro' the brain,
> Die of a rose in aromatic pain?
>
> VI.193–200

As if it were set on a great spring, the mind invariably returns to the scale of the human body no matter how far it is expanded or constricted. No sooner does the brilliant scientist withdraw her eye from her microscope than her mind instinctively follows eye and hand back to the world she knows and lives in. No sooner does Rabelais discover creatures in Gargantua's mouth than he observes them growing cabbages and playing tennis. Swift's Lilliputians never act as though they are other than life-sized humans. The mind, ever true to its first measure of things, anthropomorphizes both what it magnifies and what it miniaturizes.

The mind will not forsake the body and its senses. "The whole conduct of life," Descartes wrote, "depends on our senses, among which vision is the noblest and most universal."[12] While out of sight may not always mean out of mind, it does mean not easily kept in mind. Humans easily forget the universal whirl of particles. Technical and scientific findings, however fascinating, can quickly dissolve when they come in contact with the powerful sensations and images of everyday life.

So, in the contemporary human mind there are and always will be two kingdoms of the small: the small as defined by the human body and the small as created by science and technology. For most part, these two worlds exist independently of one another. With the exception of the psychologically aberrant (such as the compulsive handwasher and cleaner), people switch between these two worlds as mindlessly as they switch their lights off and on, or open and close their water spigots.[13]

It is not surprising that this dichotomous view does not inhibit people from going about their business. In normal times they live comfortably with ambiguity and logical inconsistency. Compartmentalization of thoughts and feelings is an ordinary and necessary activity. Thoughts follow their own tracks—and they often intersect and cross without collision. The left hand truly does not know what the right hand does—

or if it does, it does not care. The mind can achieve indifference in the face of life-sized problems. How much easier are repression and indifference in the case of the small and invisible when they are not perceived to intrude on bodily experiences, personal fate, or everlasting destiny.

Despite the growing lexicon of minute and invisible things, human beings still insist that all things be made to fit their own personal and moral narratives. Even when human beings have written the obituaries of minuscule things past and embraced infinitesimal and virtual things new, they will still fear dust's final requiem for all life. They will still dread the infinite granularity of all things, their own selves and meanings included.

NOTES

INTRODUCTION

1. J. Gordon Ogden, *The Kingdom of Dust* (Chicago: Popular Mechanics Company, 1912), 10.

2. Ibid., 10–13.

3. William Bryant Logan, *Dirt: The Ecstatic Skin of the Earth* (New York: Riverhead Books, 1995), 9.

4. Ogden, *Kingdom of Dust*, 16.

5. Cited in Logan, *Dirt*, 7.

6. C. T. Onions, *The Oxford Dictionary of English Etymology* (Oxford: Clarendon Press, 1966), 295.

7. Irving Adler estimates that "after traveling only 2,000 light-years, half of the light [from the center of the galaxy] is scattered. . . . After 4,000 years, only one-fourth of the light remains to continue the journey. . . .

After 6,000 years, only one-eighth of the light remains. . . . By the time it reaches us, after 25,000 years, the light from the center of the galaxy is so feeble that it cannot be seen" (*Dust* [New York: The John Day Company, 1958], 116).

8. They reach the upper atmosphere, where "it has been calculated that a reduction of solar radiation by twenty percent would require only $\frac{1}{400}$ of a cubic kilometer ($\frac{1}{1600}$ of a cubic mile) of a very fine-grained dust." Robert Muir Wood, *Earthquakes and Volcanoes* (New York: Weidenfeld and Nicolson, 1987), 114.

9. Ibid., 113–14.

10. Adler, *Dust*, 16.

11. For a study, see Douglas Hurt, *The Dust Bowl* (Chicago: Nelson-Hall, 1981). I used Elizabeth Bank's thoughtful summary of the work.

12. For a recent discussion of the origin of the dust storms of the 1930s, see William Cronon, "A Place for Stories: Nature, History, and Narrative," *Journal of American History* (March 1992), 1347–76.

13. The word *industry*, which comes from the French *industrie* and Latin *industria*, which connotes hard work and diligence, goes back to old Latin *indostruus*, formed from the prefix *indu* and *struere*, to build (John Ayto, ed., *Dictionary of Word Origins* [New York: Arcade Publishing, 1990], 298).

14. Over a dusty city, Adler estimated in 1958, a cubic inch of air may contain as many as fifty million dust particles. With an average size of dust particles of one micron (one-millionth of a meter) over cities, the heavier particles descend on the city as a steady rain, measured annually in hundreds and even thousands of tons. "In the city of Los Angeles, 332 tons of dust fall on every square mile in a year. In Chicago, the amount that falls on a square mile each year is 782 tons." In England, which is as dusty as the United States, "the amount of dust falling on a square mile in a year ranges from about 200 to 2,000 tons a year" (Adler, *Dust*, 92–

93). A 1970 *Encyclopaedia Britannica* article on dust suggests that about 43 million tons of dust settle on the United States per year. Of this amount, 31 million tons come from natural resources, including 1 million tons of pollen. The remainder is generated by human activities, with industry at that time being the principal contributor. Detroit, with 72 tons per month, more than doubled Los Angeles's figure of 33 tons per month. Helmut Landsberg, "Dust," *Encyclopaedia Britannica,* vol. 7 (Chicago: Encyclopaedia Britannica, 1970), 788. For data on air pollutants and their sources in the United States in 1997, see *Abstract of the United States, 1997* (Washington, D.C.: U.S. Department of Commerce, 1997), 234–35.

15. Dennis Eberl, "Clay," *McGraw-Hill Encyclopedia of Science and Technology* (New York: McGraw-Hill, 1992), 686.

16. Parodying Descartes's first proof, "I think, therefore I am," Guy Thuillier (personal communication, 1994) suggests the feminine *cogito* became "je frotte, donc je suis" (I rub and scrub, therefore I am).

17. Joseph Amato, review of Suellen Hoy's *Chasing Dirt: The American Pursuit of Cleanliness* (1995), *Journal of Social History* (Fall 1996), 277–82.

CHAPTER 1

1. Daan Smit and Nicky den Harogh, *Seeds and Fruits* (New York: Smithmark, 1996), 3–4.

2. For an overview of the hidden power of plants, see Emilio Marozzi, Francesco Mari, and Elisabetta Bertol, *Le piante magiche: Viaggio nel fantastico mondo delle droghe vegetali* (Firenze: Case Editrice Le Lettere, 1996).

3. Hippocrates proposed "excrementitious material" for numerous diseases. Galen, it might comfort the reader to know, not only advised against the pharmaceutical use of human feces but also disagreed with Xenocrates, who had recommended the internal and external use of sweat, urine,

menstrual fluid, and ear wax. Pliny praised the multiple uses of camel waste: made into ashes and combined with oil, it curls and frizzles hair; taken with drinks it cures dysentery (Theodor Rosebury, *Life on Man* [New York: Viking Press, 1969], 115–27, 35–38, 139). As late as the seventeenth century, prescriptions for scrofula included goiter oil, a concoction of ground-up newborn rats and small lizards, exposed to the sun on hot, sultry summer days. Other healing prescriptions included powders (dusts) made from toads, which were used to treat cancer of the breast, and oils of boiled frogs and earthworms, which were used "to soothe the pain of joints, nerves, and for wounds, punctures, and malign ulcers" (Piero Camporesi, *Bread of Dreams: Food and Fantasy in Early Modern Europe* [Chicago: University of Chicago Press, 1996],113).

4. Iona Opie and Moira Tatem, eds., *A Dictionary of Superstitions* (Oxford: Oxford University Press, 1989), 119–20.

5. One superstition accounted it unlucky for wedding guests to wipe off their feet anything they stepped in on the way to the wedding, while a second superstition advised keeping horse dung to bring good luck and ward off the evil eye. Others counted it good fortune to stand on a cow pie and to tread "in dog faeces without realizing it until afterwards" (ibid., 141–42).

6. The term *mummy* comes from the mountain in Persia that was the main source for this profitable trade.

7. William J. Powell, *Pillsbury's Best: A Company History from 1869* (Minneapolis: Pillsbury Company, 1985), 32.

8. For a useful work on how much the world of everyday meaning depends on metaphorical assemblage and opposition, see George Lakoff and Mark Johnson, *Metaphors We Live By* (Chicago: University of Chicago Press, 1980).

9. D. C. Winslow, "Dust," *Encyclopedia Americana*, vol. 19 (New York: Americana Corp., 1964), 427–28.

10. *Hamlet* IV.iii.9.

11. This paragraph was inspired by Ernest Becker, *Denial of Death* (New York: Free Press, 1973).

12. Douglas argues further that disorder was a chaotic jumble that defied the order of things: it was typified by birds that couldn't fly, fish that walked on the ground, and animals whose cloven hooves resembled hands. Disorder existed when improper mingling occurred between human and animals, men and women, body and food, hand and mouth (*Purity and Danger: An Analysis of the Concepts of Pollution and Taboo* [London: Routledge and Kegan Paul, 1966]).

13. Ibid., 35.

14. The Italian word *immondo*—literally translated as nonworldly—means not just dirty and filthy but immoral, corrupt, unprincipled, and evil. *Immondizia* translates as filth, rubbish, and sweepings (*Dizionario Garzanti della lingua italiana* [Milano: Garzante, 1965]). The French adjective *immonde* describes what is repulsive and disgusting. It was used to describe the taboo pig of the Old Testament and the devil himself—*l'ésprit immonde*—in the New Testament (*Petit Larousse* [Paris: Larousse, 1961]).

15. Humans naturally avoid putrescence, unless we consider fictional groups like Swift's excremental Laputan scientists or abnormal individuals like the Milwaukee cannibal Jeffrey Dahmer. *Putrid* is a synonym for *corrupt*. The Italian language links the verbs *putire, putrefare, puzzare* (to stink, to rot, to smell) and the noun *putana* (whore). Similarly, the Algonquins, a North American Indian nation, identified the prostitute with the skunk.

16. John Ayto, ed., "Dirt," *Dictionary of Word Origins* (New York: Arcade Publishing, 1990), 173. The word *manure* is not only related to *maneuver* but also affiliated with *manor* and *manual,* indicating how closely associated were excrement, agriculture, and labor in preindustrial times (ibid., 337).

17. C. T. Onions, ed., "Dirt," *The Oxford Dictionary of English Etymology* (Oxford: University Press, 1966), 271.

18. Joseph Amato, *Countryside, Mirror of Ourselves* (Marshall, MN: Crossings Press, 1981), 21–22. Peasants have been called *pariahs* (Indian) and *peons* (Spanish). Synonyms for *peasant*, in various European languages, are words literally meaning smelly, stupid, shoeless, and dirty-toed. A *villain* was a farmhand on a villa, a country estate. Also, the peasant (who by definition in French is from the *pays*, the countryside) was the antithesis of the *civilized*, the *urbane*, the *cosmopolitan*, all of which have their roots in Greek and Latin words for city. Nor was the peasant from the *court* or the *nobility*, where people were courteous and noble. Twentieth-century American slang names for country people include clod-hopper, sod buster, hayseed, hay shaker, pea picker, pumpkin peeler, stubble jumper, clover kicker, coon skinner, sorghum lapper, turnip sucker, and shit kicker. See *The American Thesaurus of Slang* (New York: Thomas Y. Crowell, 1945).

19. For the primary source of my portrait of the old order, see Joseph Amato, "A World without Intimacy: A Portrait of a Time before We Were Intimate Lovers," *International Journal of Social Sciences* 61, no. 4 (Autumn 1986): 155–68.

20. This particular essay appears in Febvre's *Life in Renaissance France* (Cambridge: Harvard University Press, 1977), 4–5. Febvre and Marc Bloch founded the French Annales school of historiography, which since the 1920s has grown to be the most influential school of history in the world.

21. Ibid., 8–9. Febvre wrote of the central place of the kitchen in the home: "The ordinary dwelling for the gentleman who was not a prince was a manor; people spent most of their time in a single room, the kitchen. Generally, meals were eaten there. (French houses almost never had a special room for dining until the eighteenth century. Even Louis XIV,

on ordinary occasions, ate his meals at a square table in front of the window in his bedroom. The nobles of the sixteenth century, having fewer pretensions, generally ate in the kitchen.) This room is called, in the dialect of some provinces, the 'heater.' That is the giveaway. It was warm in the kitchen, or at least less cold than elsewhere. There was always a fire."

22. Jerome Blum, *The End of the Old Order in Rural Europe* (Princeton: Princeton University Press, 1978), 181.

23. Camporesi, *Bread of Dreams*, 151–52.

24. For works that cast light on the human place in the biological kingdom, see Frederick Cartwright, *Disease and History* (New York: Barnes & Noble, 1972); George Forster and Orest Ranum, eds., *Biology of Man and History* (Baltimore: Johns Hopkins University Press, 1975); William McNeill, *Plagues and Peoples* (Garden City, N.Y.: Anchor, 1976); E. Wrigley, *Population and History* (New York: McGraw-Hill, 1969).

25. Joseph Lopreato, "How Would You Like to Be a Peasant?" *Human Organization* (Winter 1965): 306.

26. Emmanuel LeRoy Ladurie, *Montaillou: The Promised Land of Error* (New York: Vintage, 1979), 222, 10.

27. Ibid., 288.

28. Georges Duby, *The Early Growth of the European Economy: Warriors and Peasants from the Seventh to the Twelfth Century*, trans. Howard B. Clarke (Ithaca: Cornell University Press, 1974), 29.

29. Peter Laslett, *The World We Have Lost: England before the Industrial Age* (New York: Charles Scribner's Sons, 1965), 103.

30. Camporesi, *Bread of Dreams*, 33.

31. Eugen Weber, *A Modern History of Europe: Men, Cultures, and Societies from the Renaissance to the Present* (New York: W. W. Norton, 1971), 204–5.

32. Ackerman, *A Natural History of the Senses*, 61.

33. Norbert Elias, *History of Manners* (New York: Pantheon Books: 1978), 48.

34. Cited in Fernand Braudel, *Capitalism and Material Life, 1400–1800* (New York: Harper & Row, 1967), 122.

35. George Fatherstonaugh, *A Canoe Voyage up the Minaysotor* (St. Paul: Minnesota Historical Society, 1970), vol. 2, 69–70.

36. Arthur Young, cited in Maurice Vaussard, *Daily Life in Eighteenth-Century Italy* (New York: Macmillan, 1963), 51–52.

37. Denis Mack Smith, *Mazzini* (New Haven: Yale University Press, 1994), 21.

38. Weber, *A Modern History*, 204.

39. Gamni Salgado, *The Elizabethan Underworld* (London: J. M. Dent and Sons, 1977), 18.

40. Camporesi, *Bread of Dreams*, 152.

41. Ibid.

42. Ibid.

43. Carlo Ginzburg, *The Cheese and the Worms: The Cosmos of a Sixteenth-Century Miller* (Baltimore: Johns Hopkins University Press, 1980), 57.

44. Camporesi, *Bread of Dreams*, 55, 156–57, 159.

CHAPTER 2

1. Sidney Mintz, *Tasting Food, Tasting Freedom: Excursions into Eating, Culture, and the Past* (Boston: Beacon Press, 1996), 62.

2. For measurements in preindustrial Europe, see Witold Kula, *Measures and Men* (Princeton: Princeton University Press, 1986), and Edward Nicholson, *Men and Measures: A History of Weights and Measures, Ancient and Modern* (London: Smith, Elder & Co., 1912). For the history of weighing instruments themselves, see Charles Testus, *Mémento du pesage: Les*

instruments de pesage, leur histoire à travers les âges (Paris: Hermann & Cie, 1946).

3. Jeanne Bendick, *How Much and How Many: The Story of Weights and Measures*, rev. ed. (New York: Franklin Watts, 1989), 14, 46.

4. In *Planets, Stars and Orbs: The Medieval Cosmos, 1200–1687* (Cambridge: Cambridge University Press, 1994), Edward Grant illustrates how what he calls the medieval cosmos, "a fusion of pagan, Greek ideas, and biblical descriptions, especially the creation account in Genesis," preoccupied high medieval thought. Formulated in the twelfth and thirteenth centuries, these scholastic ideas dominated Western thought about the heavens and earth until approximately 1700. By the time rival interpretations appeared in the Renaissance and early modern period—for example Platonism, atomism, stoicism, neoplatonism, hermeticism, and especially Copernicanism—the essentially Aristotelian cosmology of scholastic thought ruled. It would continue to constitute a tradition of thinking about the heavens and the earth—setting the first premises of what we call natural science—until its final defeat at the hands of Newton's *Philosophiae naturalis principia mathematica* (1687), which marked the triumph of a view of the cosmos based on empirical observation and mathematics and which linked earth and heaven to the same laws.

5. A useful discussion of the premises of the natural sciences found in medieval thought is provided by Edward Grant, *The Foundations of Modern Science in the Middle Ages* (Cambridge: Cambridge University Press, 1996); for the freedom and tolerance of discussion and other elements that constituted "the substantive pre-conditions" of the scientific revolution, see esp. 191–205.

6. Grant, *Planets, Stars, and Orbs*, 422–33.

7. Ibid., 579, 580, 581.

8. Cited in A. C. Crombie, *The History of Science from Augustine to Galileo* (New York: Dover Publications, 1979), 45.

9. Ibid., 47.

10. Crombie offers a table of the principal sources of Western science between A.D. 500 and 1300. The range of sources on metaphysics, physics, astronomy, mathematics, medicine, plants, minerals, geology, and optics is surprising. Aside from Western works by Aristotle, Plato, Pliny, Galen, Ptolemy, Euclid, Archimedes, and, notably, Lucretius (complete text available only in 1417), Arab works by Alfardbi, Haly Abbas, Alhazen, Avicenna, and Averroës are represented (*The History of Science*, 55–63).

11. Crombie, *The History of Science*, 110. Also see David Lindberg, *Theories of Vision from Al-Kindi to Kepler* (Chicago: University of Chicago Press, 1977).

12. For examples of imaginative medieval conceptions of the afterlife see Jeffrey Russell, *Storia del Paradiso* (Roma: Editori Laterza, 1996); Jacques Le Goff, *The Birth of Purgatory* (Chicago: University of Chicago Press, 1984); Le Goff, *The Medieval Imagination* (Chicago: University of Chicago Press, 1985); and Arthur O. Lovejoy, *The Great Chain of Being: A Study of the History of an Idea* (New York: Harper and Brothers, 1936).

13. A. C. Crombie contends that what truly limited medieval science was the absence of an imperative to make actual measurements and to manipulate mathematical formulas to describe phenomena. Crombie, "Quantification in Medieval Physics," in *Changes in Medieval Society* (Toronto: University of Toronto Press, 1988), 188–207.

14. In his nineteenth-century classic, *History of Materialism* (New York: Arno Press, 1974), Frederick Albert Lange identified Pierre Gassendi, a philosopher and scientist (1592–1655), with the revival of Democritus, Epicurus, and Lucretius; direct opposition to Aristotle; and the connection of classical physics and modern atomism (vol. 1, 253–55).

15. Edward Grant argues for the importance of medieval thought as a source of modern science in the conclusion of *The Foundations of Modern Science*, esp. 191–215.

16. Robert Lenoble, *Histoire de l'idée de la nature* (Paris: Albin Michel, 1969), 259–307.

17. Ibid., 302.

18. Hugh Kearney, *Science and Change, 1500–1700* (New York: McGraw-Hill, 1971), 181.

19. Richard Kiekhefer, *Magic in the Middle Ages* (Cambridge: Cambridge University Press, 1989), esp. 133–39.

20. The phrase "subterranean physics" comes from Johann Joachim Becher, *Physicae Subterranease* (Leipzig: J. L. Gleditsch, 1703), cited in Pamela Smith's *The Business of Alchemy: Science and Culture in the Holy Roman Empire* (Princeton: Princeton University Press, 1994), 19. Smith's book offers a study of Becher (1635–82), an important alchemist and new man of his times, and his role in mingling older cosmic views with new science, economic development, and commerce at the Habsburg court.

21. Smith, *The Business of Alchemy,* 271.

CHAPTER 3

1. These examples from early fifth- to eleventh-century medieval Europe were taken from James Snyder, *Medieval Art: Painting, Sculpture, Architecture, Fourth to Fourteenth Century* (Englewood Cliffs, N.J.: Prentice-Hall, 1989); John Beckwith, *Early Medieval Art: Carolingian, Ottonian, Romanesque* (London: Thames and Hudson, 1969); and Andrew Martindale, *Gothic Art* (London: Thames and Hudson, 1967), 137.

2. Otto von Simpson, *The Gothic Cathedral: Origins of Gothic Architecture and the Medieval Concept of Order* (New York: Harper & Row, 1964), 52. Also of use in illuminating the level of fineness and delicacy expressed in cathedrals is Jean Gimpel, *The Cathedral Builders* (New York: Harper & Row, 1983).

3. This image is found in the early Christian *Apocalypse of St. Paul,* reproduced in Alice Turner, *The History of Hell* (New York: Harcourt Brace, 1993), 87.

4. Jeffrey Russell, *Storia del Paradiso* (Rome: Editori Laterza, 1996), 186, 185.

5. A. C. Crombie, "Quantification in Medieval Physics," in *Changes in Medieval Society* (Toronto: University of Toronto Press, 1988), 203–5.

6. Crombie, "Quantification," 201.

7. Cited in Jean Gimpel, *The Medieval Machine: The Industrial Revolution in the Middle Ages* (New York: Penguin Books, 1976), 149.

8. T. K. Derry and Trevor I. Williams, *A Short History of Technology: From the Earliest Times to A.D. 1900* (New York: Dover Publications, 1993), 104–13.

9. Benedetto Dei, *Cronica*, cited in Anabel Thomas, *The Painter's Practice in Renaissance Tuscany* (Cambridge: Cambridge University Press, 1995), 16.

10. Erran Wood, "The Tradition from Medieval to Renaissance," in *The History of Glass*, ed. Dan Klein and Ward Lloyd (London: Orbis, 1984), 67.

11. Benjamin Goldberg, *The Mirror and Man* (Charlottesville: University of Virginia Press, 1985), 142.

12. J. C. Margolin, "Des lunettes et des hommes, ou la satire des malvoyants au XVIe siècle," *Annales: Economies, Société, Civilisations* 30, nos. 2–3 (March–June 1975), 387. Also see Edward Rosen, "The Invention of Eyeglasses," *Journal of the History of Medicine* 11 (January and April 1956), 13–46, 183–218.

13. For a history of drawing and modeling and their definition in fifteenth-century Italy, see Robert Scheller, *Exemplum: Model-Book Drawings and the Practice of Artistic Transmission in the Middle Ages (ca. 900–ca. 1470)* (Amsterdam: Amsterdam University Press, 1995), esp. 1–17.

14. D. S. L. Cardwell, *Technology, Science and History: A Short Study of the Major Developments in the History of Western Mechanical Technology*

and *Their Relationship with Science and Other Forms of Knowledge* (London: Heinemann Educational, 1972), 27.

15. Of interest is Samuel Edgerton, "The Renaissance Development of Scientific Illustration," in *Science and the Arts in the Renaissance,* ed. John Shirley and F. David Hoeniger (Washington: Folger Books, 1985), 168–97, and James Ackerman, "Involvement of Artists in Renaissance Science," in Shirley and Hoeniger, *Science and the Arts,* 94–129.

16. Thomas, *The Painter's Practice,* 32–34.

17. A. C. Crombie, *The History of Science from Augustine to Galileo* (New York: Dover Publications, 1979), 112.

18. High Renaissance art can be conceived of as a refinement of fifteenth-century techniques, especially the mastery of mixing light and shadow in portrait painting by placing subjects around fires or near candlelight. In *High Renaissance* (New York: Penguin Books, 1975), Michael Levey writes of Correggio's *Adoration of the Shepherds*: "Here oil painting not only creates the penumbra of atmospheric darkness, through which we gradually descry further shapes and even the cool, faint glow of dawn in the distance, but the incandescent brightness from the Child is intensely conveyed by the graceful drama of light and shade" (33).

19. See Madeleine Pinault, *The Painter as Naturalist* (Paris: Flammarion, 1991).

20. For a study, see James Ackerman, "Leonardo's Eye," *Journal of Warburg and Courtauld Institutes* 41 (1978): 108–48.

21. Edward Grant, *The Foundations of Modern Science in the Middle Ages* (Cambridge: Cambridge University Press, 1996), 195.

22. George Sarton, *Six Wings: Men of Science in the Renaissance* (New York: Meridian Books, 1966), 174. Also of interest is L. S. King and M. C. Meehan, "A History of Autopsy," *American Journal of Pathology* 73 (1973): 514–44.

23. Crombie argues that "taken as a whole, medieval medicine is a

remarkable product of that empirical intelligence seen in Western technology generally in the Middle Ages" (*The History of Science*, 237).

24. In one instance, even Leonardo, behaving like teachers of medicine of the time, followed the inherited text rather than his own observations. He showed holes in the right ventricle of the heart that did not exist but that satisfied Galen's notions of how the blood circulated (Sarton, *Six Wings*, 226). For a general characterization of medieval and renaissance medicine, see Nancy Siraisi, *Medieval and Early Renaissance Medicine: An Introduction to Knowledge and Practice* (Chicago: University of Chicago Press, 1990); David Lindberg, *The Beginning of Western Science: The European Scientific Tradition in Philosophical, Religious, and Institutional Context, 600 B.C. to A.D. 1450* (Chicago: University of Chicago Press, 1992), esp. 317–68; and George Sarton, *Ancient and Medieval Science during the Renaissance, 1450–1600* (New York: A. S. Barnes and Company, 1955), esp. 7–51.

25. Leonardo da Vinci, *The Notebooks of Leonardo da Vinci* (New York: Dover Publications, 1970), vol. 2, 115, 119, 122.

26. Sarton, *Ancient and Medieval Science*, 51.

27. Marie Boas, *The Scientific Renaissance, 1450–1630* (New York: Harper and Row, 1962), 179; Allen Debus, "The Pharmaceutical Revolution of the Renaissance," *Clio Medica* 11, no. 4 (1976): 308–11; G. Urdang, "How Chemicals Entered the Official Pharmacopoeias," *Archives internationales d'Histoire des Sciences* 7 (1954): 303–4.

28. For a book based on the thesis that the discovery of the body through dissection produced a new consciousness and sensibility, see Jonathan Sawday, *The Body Emblazoned: Dissection and the Human Body in Renaissance Culture* (London: Routledge, 1995).

29. William Harvey, *The Circulation of the Blood and Other Writings* (London: J. M. Dent & Sons, 1990), 46.

30. S. Lilley, "The Development of Scientific Instruments in the Sev-

enteenth Century," *A Short History of Science: Origins and Results of the Scientific Revolution* (Garden City, N.Y.: Doubleday, 1957), 42–50. For a brief discussion of a protoindustrial revolution in the sixteenth century, and of devices and instruments that supported an emerging mechanical explanation of nature, see Hugh Kearney, *Science and Change, 1500–1700* (New York: McGraw-Hill, 1971), 40–41, 58–76.

31. Marvin Perry, *Western Civilization: Ideas, Politics, & Society* (Boston: Houghton Mifflin, 1996), 421.

32. S. Bradbury and G. L. Turner, eds., *Historical Aspects of Microscopy* (Cambridge: W. Heffer & Sons, 1967).

33. Charles Singer, *A History of Biology to about the Year 1900* (Ames: Iowa State University Press, 1989), 146–73.

34. Ibid., 161.

35. Ibid., 171.

36. Blaise Pascal, *Thoughts (Pensées)*, in Edgar Knoebel, ed., *Classics of Western Thought*, 4th ed. (New York: Harcourt Brace Jovanovich, 1988), 45.

37. In his historical survey for his "Memoir on the Organized Corpuscles Which Exist in the Atmosphere," Pasteur argued that Spallanzani's experiments were not decisive in refuting spontaneous generation, for the air he boiled could be argued to have been too damaged to allow spontaneous generation (James Conant, ed., *Pasteur's and Tyndall's Study of Spontaneous Generation* [Cambridge: Harvard University Press, 1953], 18–21).

38. Paul de Kruif, *Microbe Hunters* (New York: Pocket Books, 1962), 52.

39. Jonathan Swift, *Poetry, a Rhapsody*, 1733, cited in Singer, *A History of Biology*, 169.

40. J. William Rosenthal, *Spectacles and Other Vision Aids: A History and a Guide* (San Francisco: Norman Publishing, 1996), 39.

41. Elizabeth Bennion, *Antique Medical Instruments* (London: Sotheby Parke Bernet, 1979), 233.

42. Julius Hirschberg, *The History of Ophthalmology* (Bonn: J. P. Wayenborgh, 1982), 41.

CHAPTER 4

1. Arnold Pacey, *Technology in World Civilization* (Cambridge: MIT Press, 1990), 72.

2. Jonathan Sawday, *The Body Emblazoned: Dissection and the Human Body in Renaissance Culture* (London: Routledge, 1995), 3.

3. This basic notion is borrowed from Hugh Kearney, *Science and Change, 1500–1700* (New York: McGraw-Hill, 1971).

4. Carlo Cipolla, *Miasmas and Disease: Public Health and the Environment in the Pre-Industrial Age* (New Haven: Yale University Press, 1992), 2. Also see his *Contro un nemico invisibile: Epidemie e strutture sanitarie nell'Italia del rinascimento* (Bologna: Mulino, 1985).

5. Over time, public health institutions in Italian cities came to deal with "the quality of food on sale; the movement of beggars and prostitutes; the sanitary conditions that prevailed in the houses of poorer people; chemists' shops and the medicines they sold; sewers; hospitals; the activities of the medical profession; the sanitary condition of inns and taverns; the movements of goods, travelers, pilgrims, and ships; the quarantining of ships, travelers, and suspect merchandise; the issuing of health passes for travelers; the keeping of registers of mortality showing the name, address, and profession of the deceased and the presumed cause of death together with the medical certificates, and a hundred and one other things besides" (Cipolla, *Miasmas*, 2).

6. Ibid., 4.

7. Ibid., 5.

8. Cited in Enide Gauldie, *Cruel Habitations: A History of Working-Class Housing, 1780–1918* (London: George Allen and Unwin Ltd., 1974), 23.

9. J. H. Treble, "Liverpool Working Class Housing," in *The History of Working-Class Housing,* ed. Stanley Chapman (London: Rowman and Littlefield, 1971), 168, 185–86, 189.

10. Edwin Chadwick, *Report on the Sanitary Conditions of the Labouring Population of Great Britain,* ed. M. W. Flinn (Edinburgh: Edinburgh University Press, 1965), 319.

11. Laurence Wright, *Home Fires and Burning: The History of Domestic Heating and Cooking* (London: Routledge and Kegan Paul, 1964), 108.

12. John Ruskin, *Modern Manufacture and Design,* quoted in *Nature and Civilisation,* ed. Alasdair Clayre (Oxford: Oxford University Press, 1977), 137.

13. Charles Dickens, *The Old Curiosity Shop,* cited in Clayre, *Nature and Civilisation,* 128.

14. Alain Corbin, *The Foul and the Fragrant: Odor and the French Social Imagination* (Cambridge: Harvard University Press, 1986).

15. For a history of civic projects and engineering in the West, see Richard Kirby et al., *Engineering in History* (New York: McGraw-Hill, 1956); R. J. Forbes, *Man the Maker* (New York: Abelard-Schuman, 1958); W. H. G. Armytage, *A Social History of Engineering* (Cambridge: MIT Press, 1961); Aubrey Burstall, *A History of Mechanical Engineering* (Cambridge: MIT Press, 1965); and William Parsons, *Engineers and Engineering in the Renaissance* (Cambridge: MIT Press, 1939). For a witty discussion of sanitation from ancient times to the present, see Reginald Reynolds's *Cleanliness and Goodness* (New York: Harcourt Brace Jovanovich, 1974).

16. For an introduction to cleanliness prior to the nineteenth century, see George Vigarello, *Concepts of Cleanliness: Changing Attitudes in France since the Middle Ages* (Cambridge: Cambridge University Press, 1989).

Also of interest, to show how cleanliness was associated with manners and status, are Norbert Elias's classic *The History of Manners* (New York: Pantheon Books, 1978), and Alain Corbin's *The Foul and the Fragrant*.

17. For one suggestion out of many on the eighteenth-century search for comfort, see Witold Rybczynski, *Home: Short History of an Idea* (New York: Viking, 1986).

18. See chapter 4, "Death to Sacrifice: The Eighteenth Century Revolution against Transcendence," in Joseph Amato, *Victims and Values* (New York: Praeger, 1990), 75–102.

19. Eugen Weber, *Peasants into Frenchmen: The Modernization of Rural France, 1870–1914* (Stanford: Stanford University Press, 1976).

20. For a useful survey of new tools, materials, and technologies serving human exploration and manipulation of the small, see Marvin Kranzberg and Carroll Pursell, eds., *Technology in Western Civilization: The Emergence of Modern Industrial Society, Earliest Times to 1900* (New York: Oxford University Press, 1967).

21. Armytage, *A Social History of Engineering*, 78.

22. See Elizabeth Ewin, *Underwear: A History* (New York: Theatre Books, 1972).

23. Charles Panati, *Extraordinary Origins of Everyday Things* (New York: Harper and Row, 1987), 152–53.

24. On the origin and growth of the chemical industry, see B. G. Reuben and M. L. Burstall, *The Chemical Economy: A Guide to the Technology and Economics of the Chemical Industry* (London: Longman, 1973); F. Haber, *The Chemical Industry in the Nineteenth Century* (Oxford: Oxford University Press, 1958); American Chemical Society, *Chemistry in the Economy* (Washington, D.C.: American Chemical Society, 1973); and Stephen Mason, *A History of Sciences* (New York: Collier, 1962), 513–26.

25. From Panati's *Extraordinary Origins of Everyday Things* the following abbreviated list was assembled: chlorine bleach (Sweden, 1744), safety

razor (France, 1762), toilet paper (United States, 1857), rubber hoses (United States, 1870s), Ivory soap (United States, 1878), petroleum jelly (United States, 1879), antiperspirants (United States, 1888), shampoo (Germany, 1890s), modern hair coloring (France, 1909), paper tissue (United States, 1924), electric shaver (United States, 1931), and the nylon-bristle toothbrush (United States, 1938).

26. The French parallel to Avon was L'Oreal, which had its beginnings in 1907 when a young Parisian chemist, Eugène Schueller, responding to the passion of demimonde women for dyeing their hair, concocted an artificial dye. He made it at night in his kitchen and sold it by day to the beauty salons of Paris (Panati, *Extraordinary Origins*, 233).

27. See my review of Suellen Hoy's *Chasing Dirt: The American Pursuit of Cleanliness* in *Journal of Social History* 30 (Fall 1996): 277–80. Hoy's *Chasing Dirt* misses the technological side of the sources of the great cleanup. For an introductory essay to the vacuum cleaner, see Terry Troy, "From Sweeping to Suction," *HFD* (November 25, 1991). For the steam engine, see Richard Hills, *Power from Steam* (Cambridge: Cambridge University Press, 1989).

28. Troy, "From Sweeping to Suction," 72. Also of general use is Panati, *Extraordinary Origins*, 138–40.

29. Ewin, *Underwear*, 140.

30. For a reflective essay on materials and surfaces, see Elio Manzini, *The Material of Invention* (Cambridge: MIT Press, 1989).

31. See Robert Friedel's guide to a recent Smithsonian display, *A Material World* (Washington, D.C.: National Museum of American History, 1988) and Penny Sparke, ed., *The Plastics Age: From Bakelite to Beanbags and Beyond* (Woodstock, N.Y.: Overlook Press, 1993). On production of cement, pottery, glass, and rubber in the United States, see Victor Clark, *History of Manufacturers* (New York: McGraw-Hill, 1929), vol. 2, 492–93, vol. 3, 228–62.

32. Earl Lefshey, *The Housewares Story* (Chicago: National Manufacturers Association, 1973).

33. For a useful introduction to the notion of home as a place of intimacy and comfort, see Rybczynski, *Home*.

34. Deborah Federhen et al., eds., *Accumulation and Display: Mass Marketing: Household Goods in America, 1880–1920* (Newark, Del.: The Winterthur Museum, 1986), 15, 17.

35. See Arthur Greene, *Pumping Machines: A Treatise on the History, Design, Construction, and Operation of Various Forms of Pumps* (New York: John Wiley and Sons, 1919), esp. 1–165.

36. Asa Briggs, *Victorian Cities* (London: Penguin Books, 1968).

37. Cited in Donald Reid, *Paris Sewers and Sewermen: Realities and Representations* (Cambridge: Harvard University Press, 1991), 11.

38. For a history of New York's public water supply, see Gerald Koeppel, "A Struggle for Water," *Invention and Technology* 35 (Winter 1994): 19–27.

39. Henry Noble, *History of the Cast Iron Pressure Pipe Industry in the United States of America* (Birmingham, Ala.: Newcombe Society, 1940).

40. Joel Tarr, "Water and Wastes: A Retrospective Assessment of Wastewater Technology in the United States, 1800–1932," *Technology and Culture* 25, no. 2 (April 1984): 226–63. See also "Sewage," *McGraw-Hill Encyclopedia of Science and Technology* (New York: McGraw-Hill, 1992), 303–32.

41. Marilyn Williams, *Washing "The Great Unwashed": Public Baths in Urban America* (Columbus: Ohio State University Press, 1991).

42. For a study of the toilet as a device without fame and its inventor a prophet without honor, see Wallace Reyburn, *Flushed with Pride: The Story of Thomas Crapper* (Englewood Cliffs, N.J.: Prentice-Hall, 1969). On both sides of the Atlantic, water—the great enemy of dirt and dust—became the most important servant of advancing civilization. Washbowls,

toilets, waterworks, and fountains were springs of hope that the whole world could be as fresh and clean as pure water. "During the years 1860–1920," Stuart Galishoff writes, "American cities succeeded in developing waterworks that provided safe and plentiful water. . . . In 1880 only 30,000 Americans drank filtered water. By 1923, the only water [presumably in cities] that was not undergoing some form of filtration was the groundwater found deep in artesian wells. . . . Businessmen spearheaded the fight for improved urban water supplies, a commitment prompted by both economic necessity and civic pride" ("Triumph and Failure: The American Response to the Urban Water Supply Problem," in *Pollution and Reform in American Cities, 1870–1930*, ed. Martin Melsoi [Austin: University of Texas Press, 1980], 51).

43. See Wolfgang Schivelbusch, *Disenchanted Night: The Industrialization of Light in the Nineteenth Century* (Berkeley: University of California Press, 1988); William O'Dea, *The Social History of Lighting* (New York: Macmillan, 1958); and a Smithsonian exhibition guide, *Lighting, A Revolution: The Beginning of Electric Power* (Washington, D.C.: National Museum of American History, 1979).

44. For a study of urban lighting, see Mark Bouman, "Luxury and Control: The Urbanity of Street Lighting in Nineteenth-Century Cities," *Journal of Urban History* 14, no. 1 (November 1987): 7–37. For an expression of what lighting meant by the middle of the next century in an American city, see Louis Schrenk, "Public Lighting in Detroit: What It Is and What It Does," *The Municipal Employee* (July 1948): 15–23.

45. Cited in Schivelbusch, *Disenchanted Night*, 178.

46. Federhen et al., *Accumulation and Display*, 35.

47. Pearce Davis, *The Development of the American Glass Industry* (New York: Russell and Russell, 1949).

48. Audrey Davis and Mark Dreyfuss, *The Finest Instruments Ever Made: A Bibliography of Medical, Dental, Optical, and Pharmaceutical*

Company Trade Literature, 1700–1939 (Arlington, Mass.: Medical History Publishing Associates, 1986), 9–12.

49. Audrey Davis, *Medicine and Its Technology: An Introduction to the History of Medicine* (Westport, Conn.: Greenwood Press, 1981), esp. 183, 238–40; and Elizabeth Bennion, *Antique Medical Instruments* (London: Sotheby Parke Bernet, 1979).

50. It was no coincidence that the enemies of progress threw stones at the Crystal Palace and that critics of modernity thereafter explicitly rejected the "superficial," turning away from the bright and shiny surfaces of things. A useful introduction to the Crystal Palace is Folke Kihlstedt, "The Crystal Palace," *Scientific American* (October 1984): 132–43. In his *Notes from Underground* (1864), Dostoyevsky judged the Crystal Palace as quintessentially modern and thus quintessentially artificial.

51. On the production of soap, see B. G. Reuben and M. L. Burstall, *The Chemical Economy* (London: Longman, 1973), 12. For an analysis of the implications of marketing soap, see Vincent Vinika, *Soft Soap, Hard Sell: American Hygiene in an Age of Advertisement* (Ames: Iowa State University Press, 1992).

52. Eugen Weber, "Commonplaces: History, Literature, and the Invisible," *Stanford French Review* 4 (Winter 1980): 326.

53. Ibid., 334.

54. This phrase was borrowed from Federhen et al., *Accumulation and Display*.

55. Susan Hanson, "Home Sweet Home: Industrialization's Impact on Rural Households, 1856–1925," Ph.D. diss., University of Maryland, 1986.

56. Ibid., 201. Other factors were a decline in the hog production business, the advent of catalogues and national mail-order houses, and an increase in federal government regulation, such as the passage of the Pure Food and Drug Act. See Hanson, abstract, 2.

57. Pacey, *Technology in World Civilization*, 187.

58. Anthony Bukoski, "Polkaholics," in *Children of Strangers* (Dallas: Southern Methodist University Press, 1993), 127–44.

CHAPTER 5

1. This example was taken from Leo Lederman, *The God Particle* (New York: Dell Publishing, 1993), 20.

2. Lucretius's reflections exceeded the imagination of most people when he queried the inner nature of things: Why are some things hard and others soft? Why do some things shatter, while others ooze? How are stones polished? Why does fire burn? Why are lovers attracted by sight and smell, and why do their bodies change with the heat of passion?

3. Lucretius, *On the Nature of the Universe* (Baltimore: Penguin Books, 1951), 254–55, 256.

4. Cited in Alfred North Whitehead, *Science and the Modern World* (New York: Mentor Books, 1948), 74.

5. Cited in Charles Gillispie, *The Edge of Objectivity: An Essay in the History of Scientific Ideas* (Princeton: Princeton University Press, 1960), 255.

6. Edward Harrison, *The Mask of the Universe* (New York: Macmillan, 1985), 127.

7. Lederman, *The God Particle*, 20. Lederman himself specializes in the elusive neutrino. "Almost without properties, no mass [or very little] no electric charge, and no radius, . . . it can pass through millions of miles of solid lead with only a tiny chance of being involved in a measurable collision." In the last two decades Lederman and his kind have enumerated a collection of tiny particles. They have done this with the help of far-flung hypotheses and cyclotrons—instruments that accelerate, collide, and record the traces of ephemeral particles.

8. A team of 440 physicists, working with the world's largest collider,

the Tevatron accelerator at the Fermilab, discovered the top quark. They did this on the basis of the traces from nine out of one trillion reactions produced by the collision of proton and antiproton beams. Their discovery validated the current model of particle physics. Subatomic particles include six quarks: up and down (both found in protons); charm and strange (heavier than up and down); and bottom (heavier than strange), and the heaviest of all, top. Reversing the process of analytic disintegration, scientists have created particles of matter from ordinary light in experiments using photons generated from a laser, converting light energy into electrons and positrons ("1997–1998: A Year in Review," *Rochester Review*, Fall 1998, 33).

9. Harrison, *Mask*, 123. As imagined by twentieth-century thought, space is crisscrossed by diverse force fields and particles moving in waves and lines away from their source and toward their annihilation. Gravity— once imagined to rule a universe of straight lines, calculable distances, and constant mass—was bent to fit Einstein's curved universe and has been joined by quanta, differing movements of light, electricity, and magnetic fields in ruling the universe. Recently science has postulated gravitons "as the fundamental unit (or *quanta*) of nature thought to convey gravitational force," but as of 1992, "no graviton has ever been detected." In "Gravitons," *The Dictionary of Scientific Literacy* (New York: John Wiley and Sons, 1992), Richard Brennan suggests that gravitons serve gravity, as photons convey electromagnetism, gluons conduct the strong nuclear force, and bosons carry the weak force (131).

10. On the limits of human knowledge, John Barrow writes, "There is no reason why the Universe should be fashioned in a manner that allows human beings to discover its basic laws" (*The World within the World* [Oxford: Clarendon, 1988], 198). However, perhaps humans were fashioned by God, or experience, to understand, if only analogously, the laws of the universe out of which they have evolved.

11. "All the matter in the star [is] compressed into a region of zero volume, so the density of matter and the curvature of space-time become infinite. In other words, one has a singularity contained within a region of space-time known as a black hole" (Stephen Hawking, *A Brief History of Time: From the Big Bang to Black Holes* [New York: Bantam Books, 1988], 49).

12. Harrison, *Mask*, 123. Harrison complains that today's students "wake up when told about cells, cytoplasm, organelles, chromosomes, and the double helix, for here are things of human significance. They hear music in this litany of life-science terminology, but not in the jargon of electrons, protons, neutrons, and other lifeless creatures of the quantum world."

13. Maurice Maeterlinck, *The Life of the Ant* (New York: John Day, 1930).

14. Gillispie, *The Edge of Objectivity*, 353.

15. Howard Haggard, *Devils, Drugs, and Doctors* (New York: Harper and Brothers, 1929), 292. Nineteenth-century medical texts commonly cautioned against transfusions from dog to man. It should not be forgotten how much room there is for quackery even in the twentieth century, when contemporary medical textbooks still offer fifty causes for spitting blood, seventy causes for pain in the chest, and more than one hundred causes for coughing. Medicine, a kind of science of the invisible, is far from complete.

16. Charles Wilcocks, *Medical Advance, Public Health and Social Evolution* (Oxford: Pergamon Press, 1965), 94–95.

17. Stephen Mason, *A History of Sciences* (New York: Collier Books, 1962), 389–91.

18. Ruth Richardson, *Death, Dissection, and the Destitute* (New York: Penguin, 1988), esp. 277–79.

19. Information on medical inventions in the nineteenth century is

from "Medicine and Health," in *Great Inventions through History,* ed. Gerald Messadié (New York: Chambers, 1991), 175–88.

20. Arno Karlen, *Man and Microbes: Diseases and Plagues in History and Modern Times* (New York: Simon and Schuster, 1995), 104.

21. Sherwin Nuland, *Doctors: The Biography of Medicine* (New York: Vintage Books, 1995), 239.

22. See Eugen Weber's review of Bruno Latour's insightful but eccentric *Pasteurization of France,* in *Times Literary Supplement,* February 24–March 2, 1989, 185.

23. Bruno Latour, *The Pasteurization of France* (Cambridge: Harvard University Press, 1988), 12.

24. Cholera, whose origin is described in the earliest Sanskrit writings and has a goddess of its own in India, appeared in Europe as early as the fourteenth century. Brought by the Portuguese returning from Goa, cholera occurred in epidemic proportions in sixteenth-century Europe. Society was helpless against it. One seventeenth-century hospital regimen required patients "to drink three times daily a glass of urine of cow." They were revived from coma by pepper thrown in their eyes and the application of red-hot irons to the soles of their feet. Elsewhere, a concoction of coconut brandy distilled over horse dung was held out to the patient as the best hope (A. L. Baron, *Man against Germs* [New York: E. P. Dutton, 1957], 25).

25. Ibid., 47. As a clincher, Koch showed that cholera spread dramatically in 1892 in Hamburg, which had unfiltered water, while it was nonexistent in Altona, Hamburg's twin city on the Elbe, which filtered its water.

26. Ibid., 61.

27. "Robert Koch," *The Columbia Desk Encyclopedia,* ed. William Bridgwater and Seymour Kurtz (New York: Columbia University Press, 1963), 1145.

28. For an early stage of the elements that went into the formation, see "Germes," *Dictionnaire encyclopédique des sciences médicales,* vol. 8 (Paris: G. Masson & P. Asselin, 1882), 566–78.

29. By 1900, microbiologists knew the sources of typhoid fever, cholera, plague, undulant fever, lobar pneumonia, cerebrospinal meningitis, gonorrhea, tuberculosis, leprosy, tetanus, and diphtheria (W. D. Foster, *A History of Medical Bacteriology and Immunology* [London: William Heinemann Medical Books, 1970], 165).

30. Charles Singer, *A History of Biology to about the Year 1900* (Ames: Iowa State University Press, 1989), 459.

31. John Duffy, *The Sanitarians: A History of American Public Health* (Urbana: University of Illinois Press, 1990), 193.

32. For a discussion of nature and the sublime, see the introduction of David Nye's *American Technological Sublime* (Cambridge: MIT Press, 1994). On the size of the universe, Dale Sparling, printed lecture notes, Southwest State University, Marshall, Minn., 1996, 16.

33. Robert Hessler, *Dusty Air and Ill Health: A Study of Prevalent Ill Health and Causes* (n.p., 1912). See also Philip Drinker and Theodore Hatch, *Industrial Dust: Hygienic Significance, Measurement and Control* (New York: McGraw-Hill, 1936).

34. Mitchell Prudden, *Dust and Its Dangers* (New York: C. P. Putnam's Sons, 1903), 99–100.

35. The forensics of dust now proves important in solving crimes. Detectives once worked with suppositions, clever cross-examinations, minimal material evidence, and rudimentary science. In the second half of the twentieth century, detectives have come increasingly to rely on scientific experts and laboratories. They automatically dust for fingerprints and test for the finest traces of powders, soot, or hair. Dusts are important in identifying a body. If the science is good, the narrative convincing, and (pace all Simpson trial aficionados) the jury willing, the smallest particles

can convict. See J. L. P. Wyndham, "The Forensic Aspect of Dust," *The Criminologist*, ed. Nigel Morland (New York: The Library Press, 1972), 183–92.

36. Drinker and Hatch, *Industrial Dust*.

37. This process, which started in 1913 and continued into the 1930s, is described by its founder and main proponent, Edward Davis, in *Pioneering with Taconite* (St. Paul: Minnesota Historical Society Press, 1964).

38. More technically, integral to the experiment was crushing the rock "to a powder having no particles larger than a hundredth of an inch in diameter"; developing a process of magnetic separation of the ore in water (the machines were known as separators and cobbers); demagnetizing the ore; and transforming it through pelletizing (not sintering) into an acceptable size, since "fine ore iron can be blown out of the top of a furnace by a heavy blast of air. . . . Any particles smaller than 10 mesh—a 10-mesh screen is a sieve with 10 open spaces per linear inch—are potential flue dust." The initial crushing process reduced particles to as small as 350 mesh (ibid., 21–22, 38).

39. Any standard catalog of scientific products will confirm the primary place of measuring instruments in twentieth-century production. There are instruments and devices designed for measuring and protecting workers against poisonous gases and toxic dusts (such as a surgical bone dust collector to prevent infections). Other devices measure and regulate gases and liquids while determining their temperature, color, and other characteristics. Other instruments (which form the foundation of contemporary medicine) measure bodily functions—their regularity, output, and so forth—and chemicals, infections, and wastes.

A range of contemporary electronic devices has taken up the perennial chores of grinding, separating, distilling, demineralizing, crystallizing, and mixing. Added to such venerable measuring apparatuses as rulers, calipers, beakers, filters, balances, gauges, magnifying glasses, and microscopes, there are now devices and techniques that measure molecules and atoms, such as nuclear magnetic resonance spectroscopy and electron microscopy, which can magnify objects a million times.

40. To take three examples from the thousands of laboratories listed in the 1991 *Research Centers Directory* (2 vols., 23d ed. [Detroit: Gale Research, 1998]): the Generic Technology Center for Respirable Dust at Pennsylvania State University states its purpose to be "[the] control of the generation of micro-size respirable coal dust, including diluting, dispersing, and collecting the dust in mines, characterizing the dust, charting the interaction of dust and lungs, and exploring the relation of mine environment and geological characteristics of dust generation." The Clarkson University Center for Particulate Control in Process Equipment conducts "research in microcontamination and particulate control applied to process equipment and manufacturing." The Center for Microcontamination Control at the University of Arizona examines "surface phenomena, including studies on semiconductor manufacturing, contamination control, and solid-state physics. Projects include studies on small particle adhesion mechanisms, effects of surface contamination of small particle adhesion mechanisms, effects of surface contamination on thin film growth, theoretical studies of electromagnetic scattering from ultra fine particles, and models of clean room aerosol dynamics."

CHAPTER 6

1. Joseph Berkson, "Life Expectancy," *Encyclopaedia Britannica*, vol. 13 (Chicago: Encyclopaedia Britannica, 1970), 1091.

2. For a general history of public health in the West, see Frances Smith, *The People's Health, 1830–1910* (London: Croom Helm, 1979); George Rosen, *A History of Public Health* (Baltimore: Johns Hopkins University Press, 1993); and C. E. A. Winslow, *The Evolution and Significance of the*

Modern Public Health Campaign (New Haven: Yale University Press, 1923). For the United States, see Ralph Chester Williams, *The United States Public Health Service* (Washington, D.C.: U.S. Public Health Service, 1951); M. E. M. Walker, *Pioneers of Public Health: The Story of Some Benefactors of the Human Race* (New York: Macmillan, 1930); Mazyk Ravenel, ed., *A Half Century of Public Health*: Jubilee Historical Volume (New York: American Public Health Association, 1921); Fitzhugh Mullan, *Plagues and Politics: The Story of the United States Public Health Service* (New York: Basic Books, 1989).

For Britain, see J. H. Harley Williams, *A Century of Public Health in Britain, 1832–1929* (London: A. & C. Black, 1932); and Simon Szreter, "The Importance of Social Intervention in Britain's Mortality Decline, c. 1850–1914: A Reinterpretation of the Role of Public Health," *Social History of Medicine* 1, no. 1 (1988): 3–37.

For France, see Jean-Pierre Goubert, ed., "La médicalisation de la société française, 1770–1830," *Historical Reflections* 9, nos. 1–2 (Spring–Summer 1982); Erwin Ackerknecht, "Hygiene in France, 1815–1848," *Bulletin of the History of Medicine* 12, no. 2 (March–April), 17–55; David Lilienfeld and Abraham Lilienfeld, "The French Influence on the Development of Epidemiology," in *Times, Places, and Persons: Aspects of the History of Epidemiology* (Baltimore: Johns Hopkins University Press, 1980), 28–38; and Olivie Faure, "The Social History of Health in France: A Survey of Recent Developments," *Social History of Medicine* 3, no. 3 (1990), 437–51.

3. In the United States, the concern for workers can be seen in *Exploring the Dangerous Trades: The Autobiography of Alice Hamilton* (Boston: Little, Brown, and Company, 1943); concern for the residents of industrial America can be found in John Spargo, *The Bitter Cry of Children* (New York: Macmillan, 1909) and Jane Addams, *Twenty Years at Hull House* (New York: Macmillan, 1910).

4. The present system of school inspection did not begin until 1879 in Paris. School medical inspection in the United States began sporadically in the 1870s (Rosen, *A History of Public Health*, 341–42). An example of public health school literature from Britain prior to World War I is *School Hygiene: A Quarterly for Educationists and Doctors*.

5. Rosen, *A History of Public Health*, xxx–xxxii. For a more complex historiographical discussion of this matter, see Szreter, "The Importance of Social Intervention."

6. Anne Marie Moulin, *Le dernier langage de la médicine: Histoire de l'immunologie de Pasteur au Sida* (Paris: Presses Universitaires de France, n.d.), 41. For the compatibility of germ theory and public health, see Duffy, *The Sanitarians*, esp. 193–204.

7. Latour, *The Pasteurization of France*, 20. An 1883 British *Manual of Practical Hygiene* (New York: William Wood, 1883) illustrates public health advice on everyday life itself. Taking up matters that good taste had set aside, it commented matter-of-factly on excreta, sewers, personal hygiene, disposal of the dead, a host of diseases, disinfection, and deodorization. It also offered advice for soldiers about barracks, tents, hospitals, clothing, marching, and the transport of healthy and sick troops. The contents of the "Appendix for Americans" included separate sections on national soils, climatology, and meteorology, as well as water, ventilation, food adulteration, vital statistics, and hints to sanitary inspectors.

8. Cited in Ira Hiscock, *Preventive Medicine and Hygiene*, vol. 12 of George Blumer and Ira Hiscock, *The Practitioners Library of Medicine and Surgery* (New York: D. Appleton-Century, 1937), 308–9.

9. Ibid.

10. William Allen, *Civics and Health* (Boston: Ginn and Company, 1909).

11. Carl Harman and Lewis Bradley, *The Human Body and Its Enemies* (Yonkers-on-Hudson, N.Y.: World Book Company, 1915).

12. Ibid., iii.

13. For a timely comment on the probable cost of disease in war, see George Ellis Jones, *Hygiene and War* (Washington, D.C.: Carnegie Endowment for Peace, 1915).

14. Edward Vedder, *Sanitation for Medical Officers* (New York: Lea Febiger, 1917).

15. In *Racial Hygiene: Medicine under the Nazis* (Cambridge: Harvard University Press, 1988), Robert Proctor discusses the development and articulation of Nazi racial hygiene.

16. Naomi Rogers, *Dirt and Disease: Polio before FDR* (New Brunswick: Rutgers University Press, 1992), 13, 57.

17. Hiscock, *Preventive Medicine*.

18. Jane Delano, *The American Red Cross Text Book on Home Hygiene and Care of the Sick* (Philadelphia: Blakiston, 1933), 65. Useful for popular public health instruction in Britain was K. D. Keele's *Modern Home Nursing* (London: Oldhams Press, 1946).

19. Francis Dieuaide, *Civilian Health in Wartime* (Cambridge: Harvard University Press, 1942), 86.

20. Rosen, *A History of Public Health*, 361.

21. Lois Magner, *A History of Medicine* (New York: Marcel Dekker, 1992), 325.

22. Ibid., 326. For a review of a work that argues that U.S. resistance to the use of vaccines against tuberculosis is responsible for the current resurgence of drug-resistant tuberculosis in the United States, see Nancy Tome's review of Georgina Goldberg's *Disease and Class: Tuberculosis and the Shaping of Modern North American Society*, in *Science* 272 (May 24, 1996): 1116–17.

23. "Tuberculosis," *Columbia Desk Encyclopedia*, 2176–77.

24. Notable diseases in decline at the turn of the century were yellow fever, smallpox, typhoid, typhus fevers, malaria, and tuberculosis. At the

same time, science discovered the causes of amebic dysentery, gonorrhea, diphtheria, cholera, tetanus, gangrene, sleeping sickness, whooping cough, and syphilis (Erwin H. Ackerknecht, *A Short History of Medicine*, rev. ed. [Baltimore: Johns Hopkins University Press, 1982], 180).

25. Ackerknecht provides a list of twentieth-century Nobel laureates in medicine and physiology that illustrates how rapidly scientific discoveries contributed to an understanding of human diseases (ibid., 241–44).

26. The identification of the vectors of dengue, Rocky Mountain spotted fever, sandfly fever, and rickettsia was a partial solution of what appeared to be nature's most perplexing and important puzzle (Rosen, *A History of Public Health*, 303).

27. For the Ligue Internationale des Antivaccinateurs, the anti-vaccination league composed of English, Belgian, French, German, and Swiss doctors, see Pierre Darmon, *La longue traque de la variole* (Paris: Librairie Académique Perrin, 1986), 371–80. On the long and partially successful struggle of the nineteenth-century anti-vaccination movement in Britain, see Williams, *A Century of Public Health*, esp. 262–63.

28. For an excellent history of the washing machine, especially in France, see Quynh Delaunay, "La lavatrice," *Oggetti d'uso quotidiano: Rivoluzioni technologiche nella vita d'oggi* (Venezia: Marsilio Editori, 1998), 106–27.

29. For a short history of cosmetics and personal care, see M. C. Phillips, *More Than Skin Deep* (New York: Richard R. Smith, 1948).

30. Sulfa drugs, highly selective in their action, proved efficient in fighting many microorganisms, excepting, notably, gonococci, meningococci, viruses, rickettsia, fungi, and protozoa. Penicillin and other antibiotics proved immensely effective in treating tuberculosis, typhoid, rickettsia, dysentery, and a few viral diseases.

31. Bacteria are nature's oldest organisms and comprise the greatest number of the hundreds of thousands of species of microscopic organisms

that flourish on the earth. Countless mutants can be obtained from a single strain of bacteria. Only one in a thousand, it is estimated, is dangerous to humans; many others carry out important work within and around the body. "In the large intestine alone, a diverse community of a hundred trillion bacterial cells acts as a barrier against pathogens" (Thomas Y. Canby, "Bacteria: Teaching Old Bugs New Tricks," *National Geographic*, August 1993, 51).

32. Raymond Daudel, *The Realm of Molecules* (New York: McGraw-Hill, 1993), 31.

33. The long history of pharmacy starts in the modern West with Swiss-German Paracelsus (1493–1541), who, contemptuous of alchemists, priests, and physicians of his era, pioneered extensive chemical experiments, noted the importance of air for all living creatures, and favored the use of minerals as well as plants in medicines. Jonathan Pereira (1804–1853), one of the first teachers of pharmacy for the Royal Pharmaceutical Society of Britain, argued that the properties of chemicals could not be derived from a doctrine of signs and signatures: for example, lungwort was not good for treating lung diseases simply because the pattern of its leaves resembled lungs. Science, he argued, must actually identify the composition of plants and metals and "their dynamical properties" (M. Weatherall, *In Search of a Cure: A History of Pharmaceutical Discovery* [Oxford: Oxford University Press, 1990], 21).

CHAPTER 7

1. David Nye, *The American Technological Sublime* (Cambridge: MIT Press, 1994), 145; see especially his chapters "The Electrical Sublime," 143–72, and "The Electric Cityscape," 173–98.

2. "Light Cleaning," *Science Digest* 89 (April 1981): 27.

3. "Inspection, hospitalization, treatment with mercuric salts, potas-

sium iodide purgatives, cauterization of sores, surgical removal of parts of the penis or labia could not surely overcome any of the sexually transmitted diseases" (F. B. Smith, "The Contagious Diseases Act Reconsidered," *Social History of Medicine* 3, no. 2 [1990]: 197–216).

4. Genital herpes (which can result in serious infections) was apparently ignored and considered a relatively benign sore. Gonorrhea, which was in large part undifferentiated from other infections, was treated superficially, mistakenly understood as primarily a male disease (the signs were more obvious in males) and not as a significant source of rheumatism and infant blindness. Smith, "The Contagious Diseases Act," 214.

5. Irving Hartmann, "Dust Explosions," *Mechanical Engineers Handbook* (New York: McGraw-Hill, 1987), 7–48.

6. "Dust and Development Go Hand in Hand," *New Scientist,* September 1, 1990, 48, and Edward Goldsmith, Peter Bunyard, et al., eds., *Imperiled Planet Toxic* (Cambridge: MIT Press, 1990).

7. For Daniel Bell these elements constitute the second and third technological revolutions (the first being steam power) that have transformed Western society (Bell, "The Third Technological Revolution and Its Possible Economic Consequences," *Dissent,* Spring 1989, 164–76).

8. For a single example of the scale of new tools, see C. G. Keller and R. T. Rowe, "Hexsil Tweezers for Teleoperated Micro-assembly," *Microelectromechanical Systems* (1997): 72–77.

9. Ivan Amato, *Stuff: The Materials the World Is Made Of* (New York: Avon Books, 1998), 194–95, 234.

10. Ibid., 189.

11. Ibid., 233, 189.

12. Ninety-nine percent of electromagnetic waves escape the human eye. In its widest sense, the spectrum includes electromagnetic, acoustic, particle, and ionizing radiation but "commonly refers just to the electromagnetic spectrum, which, in order of decreasing wave length, includes

radio, microwave, infrared, visible light (which humans see), ultraviolet, X-ray, and gamma ray emissions" ("Radiation," *Columbia Desk Encyclopedia* [New York: Columbia University Press, 1967], 1759).

13. Gerald Messadié, *Great Modern Inventions* (New York: Chambers, 1991), 77.

14. Ibid., 155, 146, 144.

15. David Macaulay, *The New Way Things Work* (Boston: Houghton Mifflin, 1998), 191.

16. Richard Brennan, ed., *Dictionary of Scientific Literacy* (New York: John Wiley and Sons, 1992), 266.

17. Messadié, *Great Modern Inventions*, 141, 152.

18. A short history of the discovery of DNA is provided by James Watson, who, along with Francis Crick, deciphered the structure of DNA. See James Watson, *The Double Helix* (New York: New American Library, 1968), 80.

19. Tim Friend, "Hello Dolly! Sheep Cloning Prompts Ethical Debate," *USA Today*, February 24, 1997, 1–2.

20. Deborah Barnes, "Creating a Cloned Sheep Named Dolly," *Research in the News*, http: // science-education.nih.gov / nihHTML / ose/snapshots/multimedia/ritn/dolly/index.html. See also I. Wilmut, E. E. Schnieke, et al., "Viable Offspring Derived from Fetal and Adult Mammalian Cells," *Nature* 385, no. 6619 (February 27, 1997): 810–13.

21. Chemistry and biology in the last half of the twentieth century extended medicine's control of the small. By the 1950s, ultraviolet rays were used to treat skin infections, prevent the growth of bacteria in meat warehouses, and disinfect the water in swimming pools and the air in operating rooms (Martin Frobisher and Lucille Sommermeyer, *Microbiology for Nurses*, 9th ed. [Philadelphia: W. B. Saunders, 1956], 48). In the late 1980s, radiation's beneficial works included destroying malignant cells,

sterilizing medical products, and tracking substances through the body with radioisotopes (Charles Cobb, "Living with Radiation," *National Geographic*, April 1989, 410).

22. Thomas Canby, "Bacteria: Teaching Old Bugs New Tricks," *National Geographic*, August 1993, 41–42.

23. Cathy Newman, "Pollen of Life and Sneezes," *National Geographic*, October 1984, 501.

24. For a discussion of conodonts see Mark Purnall et al., "Conodonts and the First Vertebrates," *Endeavor* 19, no. 7 (March 1995): 20–28.

25. Newman, "Pollen," 501–2.

26. David Grimaldi, "Captured in Amber," *Scientific American*, April 1996, 84–91.

27. Georg Kleemann, "Sub-millimetre Radiotelescope Probes Universe," *Stuttgarter Zeitung* (May 9, 1992), translated in *The German Tribune*, May 22, 1992, 12.

28. Sharon Begley, "Weighing the Darkness: Unseen Matter Shapes the Universe's Fate," *Newsweek*, January 18, 1993, 44.

29. B. C. Crandall, ed., *Nanotechnology: Molecular Speculations on Global Technology* (Cambridge: MIT Press, 1996), 10.

30. "Molecular Engineering," in Crandall, *Nanotechnology*, 21.

31. Cited in Ted Kaehler, "In-Vivo Nanoscope and the 'Two-Week Revolution,'" in Crandall, *Nanotechnology*, 49.

32. Crandall, *Nanotechnology*, 31–35.

33. Flyer for 1995–1996 Ernest C. Watson Caltech Lecture Series, California Institute of Technology, Pasadena, September 1995–January 1996.

34. Gary Stix, "Waiting for Breakthroughs," *Scientific American*, April 1996, 94–99; Crandall, *Nanotechnology*, 27. See also George Whitesides, "Self-Assembling Materials," and Kaigham Gabriel, "Engineering Microscopic Machines," *Key Technologies for the Twenty-First Century*, special

book issue of *Scientific American* (New York: W. H. Freeman, 1996): 83–88, 89–94.

35. For a guide to contemporary measurement, see Herbert Klein, *The Science of Measurement: A Historical Survey* (New York: Dover Publications, 1974), 186.

36. Ibid., 264. Additionally, measures of heat, radiation, electricity, and electromagnetism have all demanded precisely calibrated units.

CHAPTER 8

1. Rachel Carson, *Silent Spring* (New York: Houghton Mifflin, 1962), 25–26.

2. Ibid., 30, 32.

3. Ibid., 169.

4. Ibid., 211.

5. Louis Battan, *The Unclean Sky* (Garden City, N.Y.: Doubleday, 1966), 3–13.

6. Jack Ferguson, "Dust in the Environments," in *The Science of Global Change*, ed. David Dunnette and Robert O'Brien (Washington, D.C.: American Chemical Society, 1992).

7. Ibid., 118.

8. Thomas Moser, Jerry Barker, and David Tingey, "Anthropogenic Contaminants," *The Science of Global Change*, 136. It is commonly claimed that ozone depletion exposes humans to harmful shortwave or ultraviolet radiation. Decreased oxidation, resulting from pollutants like methane, leaves life without air to breathe. Global warming, a consequence of rising levels of carbon dioxide exposing life to increased longwave or infrared radiation, causes human cancers, destroys vegetation, and could result in flooding from climate changes and higher ocean levels (cited in Andrew Brown's review of Al Gore's *Earth in the Balance*, "The High Price of Civilization," *Idea News* [Summer–Fall 1992], 11).

9. Richard Brennan, ed., *Dictionary of Scientific Literacy* (New York: John Wiley and Sons, 1992), 34.

10. A 1990 survey identified eighty environmental science and environmental studies programs in the United States. Charles Kuchella, "Education of Environmental Specialists and Generalists in American Universities," in Dunnette and O'Brien, *The Science of Global Change*, 477.

11. "Les maladies des victimes de Tchernobyl surprennent les spécialistes," *Le monde*, December 2, 1995.

12. "The Toxic Workplace," *City Business, Special Focus*, March 26, 1993, 9–16.

13. Laurie Garrett, *The Coming Plague* (New York: Farrar, Straus & Giroux, 1994).

14. Arno Karlen, *Man and Microbes: Diseases and Plagues in History and Modern Times* (New York: Simon and Schuster, 1995), 6.

15. See John Collinge and Mark Palmer, eds., *Prion Diseases* (Oxford: Oxford University Press, 1999).

16. Karlen, *Man and Microbes*, 6.

17. The author of *The Hot Zone* (which explores much of the same ground as *The Coming Plague*) poetically describes how scientists unsuccessfully sought the origins of Marburg (named after a German city where the disease broke out) in a cave in the vicinity of Lake Victoria. The cave—worthy of an Indiana Jones thriller—was filled with animal bones, bats, and razor-sharp crystals.

CONCLUSION

1. Blaise Pascal, *Pensées* (Baltimore: Penguin Books, 1966), 90.

2. For example, even the moth, a recondite creature of the night, is counted (at the moment there are more than 142,000 recognized species), examined, and photographed close up, with an eye to explaining chemically how moths camouflage themselves, defend themselves, kill, produce

love songs, and eat (Darlyne Murawski, "Moths Come to Light," *National Geographic*, March 1997, 41–57).

3. These purists, who would have politics and polis without passion and sin (as Nietzsche sniffed out a century ago) create an anemic regime in which intentions about being on the side of the good—the "moral cleanup"—are valued more than knowledge, courage, and action. For an examination of the modern world's attempt to control pain and suffering, see Joseph Amato, *Victims and Values: A History and a Theory of Suffering* (New York: Praeger, 1990).

4. This dual conception of purity is nicely set forth in Sidney Mintz's recent *Tasting Food, Tasting Freedom: Excursions into Eating, Culture, and the Past* (Boston: Beacon Press, 1996).

5. "In the submicroscopic, molecular, and even subatomic realms," Herbert Klein wrote in 1974, "great and continuing advances are made with microwaves, infrared and ultraviolet rays, X-rays and gamma rays. Probably," Klein continued, "the bulk of basic scientific advances of the past several score years have become possible only with the aid of such nonseeable radiations" (*The Science of Measurement: A Historical Survey* [New York: Dover Publications, 1974], 264).

6. See Robert Luky's *Silicon Dreams: Information, Man, and Machine* (New York: St. Martin's Press, 1991), esp. 390–91.

7. Brenda Laurel, "Commentary: Virtual Reality," *Key Technologies for the Twenty-First Century*, special book issue of *Scientific American* (New York: W. H. Freeman, 1996), 20.

8. David Toolan, "Praying in a Post-Einsteinian Universe," *Cross Currents* (Winter 1996–1997): 462–63.

9. For a psychological survey of the necessity of illusions to happiness, see Shelly Taylor and Jonathon Brown, "Illusion and Well-Being: A Social Psychological Perspective on Mental Health," *Psychological Bulletin* 103, no. 2 (1988): 193–210.

10. Yi-Fu Tuan, *Morality and Imagination: Paradoxes of Progress* (Madison: University of Wisconsin Press, 1989), 164.

11. A. M. Taylor, *Imagination and the Growth of Science* (New York: Schocken Books, 1967), 52–53.

12. René Descartes, *La dioptrique*, cited in A. C. Crombie, "The Mechanistic Hypothesis and the Scientific Study of Vision: Some Optical Ideas as a Background to the Invention of the Microscope," *Historical Aspects of Microscopy* (Cambridge: W. Heffer and Sons, 1967), 3–112.

13. Admittedly, a certain number of compulsive handwashers will continue to be fixated on the powers and dangers of the unseen. What may be of interest is to calculate their changing numbers and define their differing language and rituals in relation to society's changing definition of the small and lethal.

BIBLIOGRAPHIC ESSAY

A bibliography covering a thousand-year history of smallness could, however large, only be suggestive. The majority of books and articles mentioned here have already been cited in the chapter notes. I do not include a number of informal interviews I had with individuals (the most important of which are noted in the acknowledgments) who told me what dust meant to them in their work and personal lives, thus offering the vital tips which allowed me to pick my way across the infinitely vast terrain of smallness and dust.

Dust proved to be a rich subject. A standard search under the topic "dust" at the University of Minnesota yielded over a thousand entries on a range of technical subjects involving agriculture, engineering, industrial production, public health, sanitation, and safety. It also offered a sizable number of entries on dust and natural phenomena (like loess hills and volcanoes) and on dusty times and places, with the dusty and dirty 1930s leading the way.

Works from an earlier period welcomed for their comprehensive view of dust are J. Gordon Ogden, *The Kingdom of Dust* (Chicago: Popular Mechanics Company, 1912); Robert Hessler, *Dusty Air and Ill Health: A Study of Prevalent Ill Health and Causes* (n.p., 1912); Philip Drinker and Theodore Hatch, *Industrial Dust: Hygienic Significance, Measurement and Control* (New York: McGraw-Hill, 1936); and Mitchell Prudden, *Dust and Its Dangers* (New York: C. P. Putnam's Sons, 1903). Two recent useful works on dirt and dust are *Dirt: The Ecstatic Skin of the Earth* (New York: Riverhead Books, 1995); and William Rathje and Cullen Murphy, *Rubbish: The Archaeology of Garbage* (New York: HarperCollins, 1992).

Of particular use in formulating my idea of the kingdom of the small were Lucretius, *On the Nature of Things*, dedicated in 58 B.C. (Baltimore: Penguin Books, 1951); Mary Douglas, *Purity and Danger: An Analysis of the Concepts of Pollution and Taboo* (London: Routledge and Kegan Paul, 1966); Yi-Fu Tuan, *Morality and Imagination: Paradoxes of Progress* (Madison: University of Wisconsin Press, 1989); Stanley Diamond, *Primitive Views of the World: Essays from Culture in History* (New York: Columbia University Press, 1960); Mircea Eliade, *Cosmos and History: The Myth of the Eternal Return* (New York: Harper and Row, 1959); Ernst Becker, *The Denial of Death* (New York: Free Press, 1973); and George Lakoff and Mark Johnson, *Metaphors We Live By* (Chicago: University of Chicago Press, 1980).

Early in my research it dawned on me that I was on one count writing a history of science. As Arthur Lovejoy traced the shift from a hierarchical universe to an evolutionary one in *The Great Chain of Being: A Study of the History of an Idea* (New York: Harper and Brothers, 1936), and Alexander Koyré reconstructed the revolution that took Western society from a closed world to an infinite universe in his classic *From the Closed World to the Infinite Universe* (Baltimore: Johns Hopkins University Press, 1957), so my task was to tell the story of how the plain small (which for most ages was ordinary, everyday dust) became infinitely complex in modern history. On the other hand, I understood that I was tracing a parallel, though largely subsequent, history of an astronomical revolution. I was writing of the emerging and multiplying vastness and complexity of internal space. I was writing of the second infinity of the small, which Blaise Pascal intuited in his posthumously published *Pensées*, 1670 (Baltimore: Penguin Books, 1966).

However, this revolution required more than writing a history of ideas and science. It was also about the transformation of human conditions, experience, and consciousness. To understand the elemental place of dust in all traditional and particularly peasant societies, I utilized a considerable range of historical and anthropological books. An illustrative few were Theodor Rosebury, *Life on Man* (New York: Viking Press, 1969); Diane Ackerman, *A Natural History of the Senses* (New York: Vintage Books, 1995); Piero Camporesi, *Bread of Dreams: Food and Fantasy in Early Modern Europe* (Chicago: University of Chicago Press, 1996); Lucien Febvre, *Life in Renaissance France* (Cambridge: Harvard University Press, 1977); George Forster and Orest Ranum, eds., *Biology of Man and History* (Baltimore: Johns Hopkins University Press, 1975); Carlo Ginzburg, *The Cheese and the Worms:*

The Cosmos of a Sixteenth-Century Miller (Baltimore: Johns Hopkins University Press, 1980); and Fernand Braudel, *Capitalism and Material Life, 1400–1800* (New York: Harper and Row, 1967).

To grasp early medieval attempts to construct the unseen and invisibile processes, I used, among others, Edward Grant, *Planets, Stars and Orbs: The Medieval Cosmos, 1200–1687* (Cambridge: Cambridge University Press, 1994), and his *The Foundations of Modern Science in the Middle Ages* (Cambridge: Cambridge University Press, 1996); A. C. Crombie, *The History of Science from Augustine to Galileo* (New York: Dover Publications, 1979); David Lindberg, *Theories of Vision from Al-Kindi to Kepler* (Chicago: University of Chicago Press, 1977); Le Goff's *The Medieval Imagination* (Chicago: University of Chicago Press, 1985); Robert Lenoble, *Histoire de l'idée de la nature* (Paris: Albin Michel, 1969); and Hugh Kearney, *Science and Change, 1500–1700* (New York: McGraw-Hill, 1971).

For the emergence of crafts and arts from the late Middle Ages across the Renaissance into early modern history, which delivered Europeans to new levels of refinements in both seeing and manipulating the small, I utilized Jean Gimpel, *The Cathedral Builders* (New York: Harper and Row, 1983), and his *The Medieval Machine: The Industrial Revolution in the Middle Ages* (New York: Penguin Books, 1976); K. Derry and Trevor I. Williams, *A Short History of Technology: From the Earliest Times to A.D. 1900* (New York: Dover Publications, 1993); Benedetto Dei, *Cronica*, cited in Anabel Thomas, *The Painter's Practice in Renaissance Tuscany* (Cambridge: Cambridge University Press, 1995); Erran Wood, "The Tradition from Medieval to Renaissance," in *The History of Glass*, ed. Dan Klein and Ward Lloyd (London: Orbis, 1984); Edward Rosen, "The Invention of Eyeglasses," *Journal of the History of Medicine* 11 (January and April, 1956): 13–46, 183–218; and, for more on glasses, Alberto Manguel, *A History of Reading* (New York: Viking, 1996), 291–306. Also valuable were Robert Scheller, *Exemplum: Model-Book Drawings and the Practice of Artistic Transmission in the Middle Ages (ca. 900–ca. 1470)* (Amsterdam: Amsterdam University Press, 1995), esp. 1–17; D. S L. Cardwell, *Technology, Science and History: A Short Study of the Major Developments in the History of Western Mechanical Technology and Their Relationship with Science and Other Forms of Knowledge* (London: Heinemann Educational, 1972); and Melvin Kranzberg and Carroll Pursell, eds., *Technology in Western Civilization*, 2 vols. (New York: Oxford University Press, 1967).

Measurements and their refinement in preindustrial Europe were crucial to the order of things, as can be grasped from A. C. Crombie, "Quantification in Medieval Physics," in *Changes in Medieval Society* (Toronto: University of Toronto Press, 1988); Witold Kula, *Measures and Men* (Princeton: Princeton University Press, 1986); Herbert Klein, *The Science of Measurement: A Historical Survey* (New York: Dover Publications, 1974); and Edward Nicholson, *Men and Measures: A History of Weights and Measures, Ancient and Modern* (London: Smith, Elder and Co., 1912).

For the history of weighing instruments themselves, see Charles Testus, *Mémento du pesage: Les instruments de pesage, leur histoire à travers les âges* (Paris: Hermann & Cie, 1946); Jeanne Bendick, *How Much and How Many: The Story of Weights and Measures*, rev. ed. (New York: Franklin Watts, 1989); and Alfred Crosby, *The Measure of Reality: Quantification and Western Society, 1250–1600* (Cambridge: Cambridge University Press, 1997).

Of parallel importance to measurement was illustration, on which craftsmen, artists, anatomists, naturalists, and explorers depended. Of relevance to this subject are Samuel Edgerton, "The Renaissance Development of Scientific Illustration," in *Science and the Arts in the Renaissance,* ed. John Shirley and F. David Hoeniger (Washington, D.C.: Folger Books, 1985), 168–97; James Ackerman, "Leonardo's Eye," *Journal of Warburg and Courtauld Institutes* 41 (1978): 108–48; and Leonardo da Vinci, *The Notebooks of Leonardo da Vinci,* 2 vols. (New York: Dover Publications, 1970), vol. 2, 115, 119, 122. For an illustrated book of the artist as naturalist, see Madeleine Pinault, *The Painter as Naturalist* (Paris: Flammarion, 1991).

For a general characterization of medieval and renaissance medicine, see Nancy Siraisi, *Medieval and Early Renaissance Medicine: An Introduction to Knowledge and Practice* (Chicago: University of Chicago Press, 1990); David Lindberg, *Beginnings of Western Science: The European Scientific Tradition in Philosophical, Religious, and Institutional Context, 600 B.C. to A.D. 1450* (Chicago: University of Chicago Press, 1992); George Sarton, *Ancient and Medieval Science during the Renaissance, 1450–1600* (New York: A. S. Barnes and Company, 1955); Jonathan Sawday, *The Body Emblazoned: Dissection and the Human Body in Renaissance Culture* (London: Routledge, 1995); and S. Lilley, "The Development of Scientific Instruments in the Seventeenth Century," *A Short History of Science: Origins and Results of the Scientific Revolution* (Garden City, N.Y.: Doubleday, 1957), 42–50.

For a brief discussion of devices and instruments that supported the emerging mechanical explanation of nature, see Hugh Kearney, *Science and Change, 1500–1700* (New York: McGraw-Hill, 1971); S. Bradbury and G. L. Turner, eds., *Historical Aspects of Microscopy* (Cambridge:

W. Heffer and Sons, 1967); Elizabeth Bennion, *Antique Medical Instruments* (London: Sotheby Parke Bernet, 1979); Julius Hirschberg, *The History of Ophthalmology* (Bonn: J. P. Wayenborgh, 1982); and William Rosenthal, *Spectacles and Other Vision Aids: A History and a Guide* (San Francisco: Norman Publishing, 1996).

For civilization itself to be cleaned up and put in control of the emerging microcosm, unprecedented machines, materials, and goods had to be supplied to society at large. Indeed, the industrial world, which ground out so much dust and made it into distinct particulates characterizing cities and skylines, was the defining event in altering human relations to small, fine, and eventually invisible things. For works offering distinct insights and vistas into this immense transformation, see Enide Gauldie, *Cruel Habitations: A History of Working-Class Housing, 1780–1918* (London: George Allen and Unwin Ltd., 1974); Edwin Chadwick, *Report on the Sanitary Conditions of the Labouring Population of Great Britain*, ed. M. W. Flinn (Edinburgh: Edinburgh University Press, 1965); and Laurence Wright, *Home Fires and Burning: The History of Domestic Heating and Cooking* (London: Routledge and Kegan Paul, 1964), 108.

The roles of technology, engineering, and public projects in the industrial transformation are found in Arnold Pacey, *Technology in World Civilization* (Cambridge: MIT Press, 1990); Richard Kirby et al., *Engineering in History* (New York: McGraw-Hill, 1956); R. J. Forbes, *Man the Maker* (New York: Abelard-Schuman, 1958); W. H. G. Armytage, *A Social History of Engineering* (Cambridge: MIT Press, 1961); and Aubrey Burstall, *A History of Mechanical Engineering* (Cambridge: MIT Press, 1965).

For a useful survey of new tools and technologies serving the advancing exploration and manipulation of the small, see Marvin Kranzberg and Carroll Pursell, eds., *Technology in Western Civilization: The Emergence of Modern Industrial Society, Earliest Times to 1900* (New York: Oxford University Press, 1967); and F. Haber, *The Chemical Industry in the Nineteenth Century* (Oxford: Oxford University Press, 1958).

New machines and materials lay at the heart of the revolution. For information on the steam engine and pumps, see Richard Hills, *Power from Steam* (Cambridge: Cambridge University Press, 1989); Arthur Greene, *Pumping Machines: A Treatise on the History, Design, Construction, and Operation of Various Forms of Pumps* (New York: John Wiley and Sons, 1919); and Henry Noble, *History of the Cast Iron Pressure Pipe Industry in the United States of America* (Birmingham, Ala.: Newcombe Society, 1940). For a reflective essay on water and dust-repellent materials and surfaces, see Elio Manzini, *The Material of Invention* (Cambridge: MIT Press, 1989); Robert Friedel's guide to a recent Smithsonian display, *A Material World* (Washington, D.C.: National Museum of American History, 1988); and Penny Sparke, ed., *The Plastics Age: From Bakelite to Beanbags and Beyond* (Woodstock, N.Y.: Overlook Press, 1993). For a history of glass, see Pearce Davis, *The Development of the American Glass Industry* (New York: Russell and Russell, 1949).

Medicine accounted for some of the finest precision tools and machines. For an introduction to this subject, see Audrey Davis and Mark Dreyfuss, *The Finest Instruments Ever Made: A Bibliography of Medical, Dental, Optical, and Pharmaceutical Company Trade Literature, 1700–*

1939 (Arlington, Mass.: Medical History Publishing Associates, 1986), 9–12; and Audrey Davis, *Medicine and Its Technology: An Introduction to the History of Medicine* (Westport, Conn.: Greenwood Press, 1981), esp. 183, 238–40.

The cleanup altered cities, starting with their supply and utilization of water, as shown by Asa Briggs, *Victorian Cities* (London: Penguin Books, 1968); Donald Reid, *Paris Sewers and Sewermen: Realities and Representations* (Cambridge: Harvard University Press, 1991); Joel Tarr, "Water and Wastes: A Retrospective Assessment of Wastewater Technology in the United States, 1800–1932," *Technology and Culture* 25, no. 2 (April 1984): 226–63. Also of use is "Sewage," *McGraw-Hill Encyclopedia of Science and Technology* (New York: McGraw-Hill, 1992), 303–32; Marilyn Williams, *Washing "The Great Unwashed": Public Baths in Urban America* (Columbus: Ohio State University Press, 1991); Stuart Galishoff, "Triumph and Failure: The American Response to the Urban Water Supply Problem," in *Pollution and Reform in American Cities, 1870–1930,* ed. Martin Melsoi (Austin: University of Texas Press, 1980); and Wallace Reyburn, *Flushed with Pride: The Story of Thomas Crapper* (Englewood Cliffs, N.J.: Prentice-Hall, 1969).

If the control of water is one side of the great cleanup, the development and utilization of light is the other. For a few guides to this subject, see Wolfgang Schivelbusch, *Disenchanted Night: The Industrialization of Light in the Nineteenth Century* (Berkeley: University of California Press, 1988); William O'Dea, *The Social History of Lighting* (New York: Macmillan, 1958); and Mark Bouman, "Luxury and Control: The Urbanity of Street Lighting in Nineteenth-Century Cities," *Journal of Urban History* 14, no. 1 (November 1987): 7–37.

For an introduction to cleanliness, an ideal that drove the transformation of body and society at the same time that industry provided the engine, materials, and goods, see George Vigarello, *Concepts of Cleanliness: Changing Attitudes in France since the Middle Ages* (Cambridge: Cambridge University Press, 1989); and Reginald Reynolds's *Cleanliness and Godliness* (New York: Harcourt Brace Jovanovich, 1974). Also of interest, to show how much cleanliness was associated with manners and status, are Norbert Elias's classic *History of Manners* (New York: Pantheon Books, 1978) and Alain Corbin, *The Foul and the Fragrant: Order and the French Social Imagination* (Cambridge: Harvard University Press, 1986).

Histories of diverse dimensions of the cleanup of everyday life are suggested by Charles Panati, *Extraordinary Origins of Everyday Things* (New York: Harper and Row, 1982); Henry Petroski, *The Evolution of Useful Things* (New York: Vintage Books, 1992), and his *The Pencil: A History of Design and Circumstances* (New York: Alfred Knopf, 1993); Elizabeth Ewin, *Underwear: A History* (New York: Theatre Books, 1972); Suellen Hoy, *Chasing Dirt: The American Pursuit of Cleanliness* (New York: Oxford University Press, 1995); Earl Lefshey, *The Housewares Story* (Chicago: National Manufacturers Association, 1973); Deborah Federhen et al., eds., *Accumulation and Display: Mass Marketing: Household Goods in America, 1880–1920* (Newark, Del.: The Winterthur Museum, 1986; Eugen Weber, "Commonplaces: History, Literature, and the Invisible," *Stanford French Review* 4 (Winter 1980): 315–34; Susan Hanson, "Home Sweet Home: Industrialization's Impact on Rural Households, 1856–1925," Ph.D. diss., University of Maryland, 1986; and Vincent Vinika, *Soft Soap, Hard Sell: American Hygiene in an Age of Advertisement* (Ames: Iowa State University Press, 1992).

As technology and industry created the capacities to banish dirt and darkness and produce fine and small goods in mass quantity, theoretical science opened the door to the entirely unexplored cosmos of atom and microbe. To grasp the dimension of this revolution, see Philip Morrison and Phylis Morrison, *Powers of Ten* (San Francisco: Scientific American Library, 1982); Alfred North Whitehead, *Science and the Modern World* (New York: Mentor Books, 1948); and Charles Gillispie, *The Edge of Objectivity: An Essay in the History of Scientific Ideas* (Princeton: Princeton University Press, 1960), 255.

For twentieth-century physics of the small, see Bernard Pullman, *The Atom and the History of Human Thought* (Oxford: Oxford University Press, 1998); Leo Lederman, *The God Particle* (New York: Dell Publishing, 1993); Edward Harrison, *The Mask of the Universe* (New York: Macmillan Publishing Company, 1985); John Barrow, *The World within the World* (Oxford: Clarendon, 1988); Bruce Gregory, *Inventing Reality: Physics as Language* (New York: John Wiley and Sons, 1988); and Stephen Hawking, *A Brief History of Time: From the Big Bang to Black Holes* (New York: Bantam Books, 1988).

For emerging microworlds in chemistry, biology, and medicine, see Stephen Mason, *A History of Sciences* (New York: Collier Books, 1962); Raymond Daudel, *The Realm of Molecules* (New York: McGraw-Hill, 1993); Gerald Messadié, ed., *Great Inventions through History* (New York: Chambers, 1991), 175–88; and Joel Howell, *Technology in the Hospital: Transforming Patient Care in the Early Twentieth Century* (Baltimore: Johns Hopkins University Press, 1995).

On the world of man and microbes specifically, see Arno Karlen, *Man and Microbes: Diseases and Plagues in History and Modern Times* (New York: Simon and Schuster, 1995); Sherwin Nuland, *Doctors: The*

Biography of Medicine (New York: Vintage Books, 1995); Hans Zinsser, *Rats, Lice, and History* (Boston: Little, Brown, 1935); and A. L. Baron, *Man against Germs* (New York: E. P. Dutton, 1957). Also see W. D. Foster, *A History of Medical Bacteriology and Immunology* (London: William Heinemann Medical Books, 1970).

The teachers of this microcosmic order were the proponents of public health, who over a couple decades argued whether dust and dirt or germs held the key to disease. For a few works on public health, see Charles-Edward Winslow, *The Conquest of Epidemic Disease: A Chapter in the History of Ideas* (Princeton: Princeton University Press, 1943); Frances Smith, *The People's Health, 1830–1910* (London: Croom Helm, 1979); George Rosen, *A History of Public Health* (Baltimore: Johns Hopkins University Press, 1993); Fitzhugh Mullan, *Plagues and Politics: The Story of the United States Public Health Service* (New York: Basic Books, 1989); Alan Kraut, *Silent Travelers: Germs, Genes, and the Immigrant Menace* (Baltimore: Johns Hopkins University Press, 1994); Olivie Faure, "The Social History of Health in France: A Survey of Recent Developments," *Social History of Medicine* 3, no. 3 (1990): 437–51; and F. B. Smith, "The Contagious Diseases Act Reconsidered," *Social History of Medicine* 3, no. 2 (1990): 197–216.

In the United States, the growing interest in workers' safety can be seen in Alice Hamilton, *Exploring the Dangerous Trades* (Boston: Little, Brown, 1943); concern for the residents of industrial America can be found in John Spargo, *The Bitter Cry of Children* (New York: Macmillan, 1909), and Jane Addams, *Twenty Years at Hull House* (New York: Macmillan, 1910). Specifically revealing the convergence of germ theory and anti-immigrant prejudice is Naomi Rogers, *Dirt and Disease: Polio before FDR* (New Brunswick: Rutgers University Press, 1992).

Of course, medical advance was paralleled by increasing control of all facets of the environment of industrial society, as suggested by such books as Virginia Scott Jenkins, *The Lawn: A History of an American Obsession* (Washington, D.C.: Smithsonian Institution Press, 1994); David Nye, *The American Technological Sublime* (Cambridge; MIT Press, 1994); Ivan Amato, *Stuff: The Materials the World Is Made Of* (New York: Avon Books, 1998); and Gerald Messadié, *Great Modern Inventions* (New York: Chambers, 1991).

At accelerating rates, science penetrated the inner recesses of life with work on genetics, as outlined by James Watson, *The Double Helix* (New York: New American Library, 1968). For the controversy generated by the recent cloning of the sheep Dolly, see I. Wilmut, E. E. Schnieke, et al., "Viable Offspring Derived from Fetal and Adult Mammalian Cells," *Nature* 385, no. 6619 (February 27, 1997): 810–13, and Deborah Barnes, "Creating a Cloned Sheep Named Dolly," *Research in the News,* http://science-education.nih.gov/nihHTML/ose/ snapshots/multimedia/ritn/dolly/index.html. And for biological engineering, see Michael Russ and Roger Straughan, *Improving Nature? The Science and Ethics of Genetic Engineering* (Cambridge: Cambridge University Press, 1996).

Technology continues to expand and refine its capacity to manipulate the molecular and atomic worlds, as suggested by B. C. Crandall, ed., *Nanotechnology: Molecular Speculations on Global Technology* (Cambridge: MIT Press, 1996); and George Whitesides, "Self-Assembling Materials," and Kaigham Gabriel, "Engineering Microscopic Machines," both in *Key Technologies of the Twenty-First Century,* special book issue of *Scientific American* (New York: W. H. Freeman, 1996), 83–88, 89–94. Also of interest is Thomas Hankins and Robert Silverman, *Instruments and the Imagination* (Princeton: Princeton University Press, 1995).

Obviously, the processing, transforming, and utilizing of such immense amounts of matter have produced deadly particulates around the globe. A few representative works on this subject are Edward Goldsmith, Nicholas Hildyard, et al., *The Imperiled Planet: Restoring Our Endangered Ecosystems* (Cambridge: MIT Press, 1990); Richard Sommerville, *The Forgiving Air: Understanding Environmental Change* (Berkeley: University of California Press, 1996); Jack Ferguson, "Dust in the Environments," in *The Science of Global Change,* ed. David Dunnette and Robert O'Brien (Washington, D.C.: American Chemical Society, 1992); and, for a dawning concern of the 1990s, "The Toxic Workplace," *City Business, Special Focus,* March 26, 1993, 9–16.

The threat of the small has been enhanced and made vivid by the resistance of traditional diseases and the appearance of sinister maladies that attack the immune system itself. These have become the object of several recent books, including Laurie Garrett, *The Coming Plague* (New York: Farrar, Straus and Giroux, 1994); Stephen Hall, *A Commotion in the Blood: Life, Death, and the Immune System* (New York: Henry Holt and Company, 1997); and Michael Oldstone, *Viruses, Plagues, and History* (New York: Oxford University Press, 1998). Yet the small, which nurtures fear and terror, paradoxically also remains a matter of confident control and expanding hope. It is a kind of last frontier evoking both unprecedented promises and primal fears and images.

Conceiving the small continues to provoke and puzzle human thought. It invites us to visualize a host of invisible things, a myriad imagined things, and machine-made images and tracings. It brings us, if we dare speculate, into confrontation with "the second infinity" that so terrified Pascal. It leads us either to believe in a God who guides all things, however minute, or to postulate atoms—kernels of destiny like those of Lucretius—whose remorseless nature displaces any hope in God or fear of death. Contemporary science, and technology in particular, imposes a different kind of smallness. Its knowledge and control, on which we blindly depend for our well-being and abundance, is conditional on the finest machines and subtlest conjectures. None of us—as Henry Adams made clear in his *Education* (1917)—can keep apace with the emerging infinity of the whirling and splitting atom. The small presses in on us as never before. We gaze at its sundry forms, without a clue about their implications, filled with elemental fears and hopes, dependent on the oldest metaphors, while earnest and insistent on our basic wants. The infinity of the small has arrived.

PERSONAL THOUGHTS
AND THANKS

Each family has its own history of dust. When I began thinking about writing this book, I asked everyone I met about their relation to dust—dust on the body, at work, at home, in the street. Many responded imaginatively and intelligently, but none as well as my mother. With a wonderful memory for detail, this talkative woman—who my father said never forgets anything—became truly loquacious. She left no rug unturned in her effort to tell me all she knew about dust and eliminating it.

My mother made it clear to me that each generation of our family had a different experience with dust. She told me about the dust her parents from Wisconsin encountered, working among the paper mills of the Fox River Valley. She ventured to guess how my father's parents experienced the dusts of Sicily, when they followed their donkeys up worn mountain paths, worked with stone, and stood under the raining soot and ash of Mt. Etna. She described the new dusts they must have encountered when they immigrated to the anthracite coal mining region of Pennsylvania, where blackened men returned from the mines to homes nestled between heaps of stone and coal dust. My mother recollected from visits to my father's cousins in the small Pennsylvania village of Kelayres that coal dust pervaded their houses, gathered in the gutters of the village's few paved streets and in the garden soils, etched itself into people's grimy skins, and was coughed up in the mucus of old wheezing men.

Her parents encountered new dusts—dusts my mother's family would come to know as well—when they moved to Detroit, Michigan, where each industry had its own smoke and dust: gray and black smokes from heating plants, red smoke from metal foundries, and various colors of smoke from down-river chemical plants. The scraping and building of new roads and public waterworks added to the dusts of this booming city. Near the railroad tracks and factories, coal dusts and metal tailings dominated. In the city of the automobile, an abundance of greases and oils turned dusts grimy. According to my mother, each blue-collar worker—foundry worker, grain miller, or cigar roller—returned home wearing dust to match the trade.

Being clean meant an awful lot to my mom and dad. At age seven my dad sold fruit to factory workers out of a cart pulled by a horse his stepfather kept in the garage. At age ten he worked in the Italian store at Eastern Market, where smells, sounds, and dust abounded. When he graduated from high school at sixteen, he got a job at Western

Union. There he learned to wear white shirts, sported two-tone shoes, and kept his first car spotlessly clean. When he and my mom dated, they loved to drive down to the Detroit River. Along the way they would pass the city's great waterworks, which as much as anything stood for—in fact, accounted for—a new city of bright and shiny people. They would drive, as the young and courting did, over the bridge to Belle Isle, at whose center stood the wonderful Scott Fountain with its colored water, and then they would drive out along the Detroit River five or six miles to Grosse Pointe, where the new rich industrialists escaped from the dust and din of the city they were building.

My mother recalled her work as a saleswoman at a five-and-dime. At the end of the day, she threw oiled sawdust on the floor to sweep up. She covered all the counters with blankets, except for the candy and food counters, which she covered with cheesecloth to keep the flies off. She cleaned the few glass counters the store had with a mixture of vinegar and water, adding baking soda for polish. She used a feather duster on the boxes of merchandise. Frequent visits by the city health inspector encouraged the store owners to keep the bathrooms and food up to standards.

Married in 1937, my mom had the first home of her own on the east side of Detroit in 1941. As the young wives of her generation did, she took pride in her battles against dust, dirt, and darkness. She felt superior to her relatives in the Michigan and Wisconsin countryside because they were still without running water, electric lights, paved streets, and lawns. She was committed to a daily and lifelong war against dust and dirt. Her arsenal comprised a big broom, a whisk broom, brushes of all sorts (some bought from the Fuller Brush man), and rags (occasionally purchased by the bagful when no old sheets or clothes were available from the Salvation Army). Mops, buckets, squeegees, sponges, and chamois, cleansers, bleaches, and detergents added to her weaponry. She even had bubble bath to please and clean her only son, who was usually filthy after a hard day of fighting World War II in the foxholes of nearby fields and on the dusty mounds of building sites.

Trade names were a part of her household language. I remember Ajax Cleaner and Roman Cleanser most. But there were also Duz, Tide, Lifebuoy soap, Spic & Span, and Fels Naphtha. Lava soap, which purportedly contained grains of volcanic pumice, was used by my grandfather, a factory worker at Hudson Motor, to wash his large and grimy hands, whose size, strength, and capacity to make things I so admired.

More than once a week my mother hung out laundry and shook out her throw rugs at the front and back doors. She vacuumed her living and dining room rugs twice a week with a stand-up cleaner that roared and had headlights that shone on the dirt. She beat her rugs seasonally and washed them annually with soap and a Turkish towel, whose rough surface picked up the hair, lint, and dirt that filled the carpets' nap. She always seemed to be washing the oilcloth that covered our small kitchen table, especially to remove crumbs from our burnt toast. At least once a week, she washed the linoleum kitchen floor and the stairs that led to the back door landing and the basement.

My mother also had her annual cycles of cleaning. Spring cleaning was thorough, but Christmas cleaning was extra-special because all our relatives came to our house. Rugs were cleaned especially well, furniture oiled, glass polished, and—the biggest job of all—the icicle crystals on the small four-tiered chandelier that hung above the dining room table were soaked and polished.

I remember one day in my parents' bedroom seeing tiny dust particles rising and falling at the window. I marveled at their shining multitudes. They gently rose and fell, darted up and down, vanished and reappeared until I grew tired of watching them. That was the first time I noticed dust's silvery dance. My mother, who when dressed up smelled of invisible perfumes and sported shiny sequins, was another epiphany. She was the most sparkling of queens. In my eyes, she stood like an angel beyond the filth, dirt, and dust she campaigned against day in and day out.

At the head of our basement, a serious theater in my mother's war against dirt, stood an electric washer with a movable wringer, two great washtubs, and a metal scrub board. Nearby a small ironing board for ironing sleeves and collars rested on top of a larger board. In the middle of the basement was the central drain. Once, insisting she could clean it better than my father could, she abruptly yanked on his metal snake and got a face full of slimy scum. The back of the basement held a coal furnace, a coal bin, and a metal coal chute. Our furnace, however, had none of the pristine terror of my friend's larger and automatically fed furnace, which produced silver buckets full of cinders, large clinkers, and the finest dusts, which he had to haul out all winter long. Nevertheless, our forced-air furnace blew its share of soot and dirt into the registers and accounted for much of the lint that drifted across the ceiling and into the corners of the house.

My mom explained that a revolution occurred in the basement when my dad installed a gas furnace just after the war. He partitioned the basement and built a whole room around it. In the "furnace room," he built a storage closet, a can cellar, and a large workspace at whose center was his tidy workbench. He always brushed off the wood and metal shavings and sawdust, and sometime in the early fifties he placed a fluorescent light above it.

Cleaning and tidying up were the ways my father imposed order on the world. My mother didn't need to remind me that he always hung up his clothes as soon as he came home from work. He kept his closet in perfect order and always straightened the money in his wallet. He never did yard or housework without putting on work clothes. He changed the screens and storm windows as the seasons required, and he always had the right brushes and brooms for cleaning the screens and scraping wood and the proper sponges and chamois to clean the glass. He also had an industrial broom he used for the garage and the sidewalk. He applied a second coat of paint to everything he painted.

My mother admits that keeping my neat and tidy father clean was not a big job. Of course, she regularly washed and ironed his clothes and took his suits to the cleaners. But compared to the factory workers, who worked around the clock to build the arsenal of democracy, he was as clean as a whistle. He took a bath twice a week, he didn't need to wear deodorants, and, as my mother claimed truthfully, his feet didn't stink like those of her side of the family.

I posed a more difficult problem. There was no clothing, however new, in which I wouldn't play if given a chance. I was often covered with grass stains from wrestling on the lawn. My friends and I liked digging in the fields behind our houses, playing on our gravel schoolyard, and sliding into bases on the dusty baseball diamonds. We ran up and down the dusty limestone alleys, where from time to time the rats had to be exterminated by fumigation. Once a week a solitary ragman came down the alley with a nag of a white horse and a great silver horn whose bellow reminded us all that if we were not good we would be hauled away with the trash.

Fortunately for my mom, she didn't have to fight me to take a bath. She taught me to take pride in the great ring of dirt I left around the tub. My thick-coated Canadian shepherd dog, Spikes, needed cleaning too: we fought his fleas, pulled burrs from his coat, and occasionally found a tick. We gave him a washing in the basement tub when he smelled too much like the dog he was.

Mom not only had to clean me and my dog, but she also had to cope with my illnesses and heal my dirty war wounds. She battled many of them with words: "The more it hurts, the better it heals." On bad infections she poured hydrogen peroxide, and together we peered into the fizzing brine to see the discharge of the infecting particles. She was a master at getting dust and dirt out of my eyes and ears. One night she fought a battle against my greatest earache, which resulted from a sand fight at the beach. Her vigil lasted almost all night. She poured hot oils in my ear and blew smoke from a cigarette into the ear canal, even though she didn't smoke. By morning she had evicted all the sand, and I was ready to play again. My mother cured athlete's foot and poison ivy and carried on a lengthy fight against pinworms. Though I was spared impetigo, I did not escape ringworm—which she blamed on movie seats. She shaved my hair, applied some salve, drew a ring of Mercurochrome around it, and sent me off to school crowned by a cap made out of one of her nylon stockings cut in half and tied on the top. The treatment killed the ringworm, but I nearly died of humiliation.

Mom had me inoculated when I needed to be. She made me aware from a very early age that there were small things in the world called germs that were far more deadly than my pinworms. Perhaps my mother was more aware of the dangers of dust and dirt than most of her peers because her favorite aunt, May, had served as a nurse in World War I and fought the great influenza epidemic of 1918, which killed more than twenty million people in the United States and Europe. After the war, May became a Detroit public health nurse. May was really germ-conscious, my mother said: "She would make me wash my hands until they were wrinkled and it hurt under my nails. She told me I'd get sick if I didn't."

My mother was germ-conscious too. She cautioned me to wash my hands before I ate and to pay attention to what I was picking up and putting in my mouth. (But she also told me, "You'll eat a peck of dirt before you die, and it's good for you.") From early on, I knew that within and beyond dust lurked invisible, lethal enemies. I knew these germs could exist anywhere—in the air and water, on the ground, in food, on skin, and in mouths. While germs were not quite the wax in my ears, the dirt under my fingernails and between my toes, or the mucus from my nose, in my mind they were tied up with cleanliness. In my childhood imagination, germs were an invisible world linked in confusing ways to the visible world. My mother reminded me of the time when I was very young and bent over to pick up a prophylactic. She scolded, "Don't touch it. It's a poison Japanese balloon." I identified the invasion of poison balloons with the ominous red lantern that stood in our neighbor's backyard to fight off Japanese beetles. I concluded that the Japanese must be the sneakiest of enemies, master of the sinister invisible. My uncle Sam returned home from the war, married my Aunt Milly, and before they had a child started to die of stomach cancer. It invaded his body, turning a husky man into an emaciated creature. When I visited him, I religiously drank out of a clean glass without once needing to be reminded. I did not want to be taken by his unseen killer.

Nevertheless, this germ-consciousness didn't stop me or my friends from picking up candy off the ground, wiping it along our pants, and eating it, or sharing licks from ice cream cones or drags from cigarettes. We pricked our fingers and, commingling our blood, swore eternal bonds. We chewed tobacco, held farting and pissing contests, and played mumblety-peg, a knife game that concluded with the loser trying to extract from the dirt a sharpened peg each of the winners had driven into the ground with three hard blows of his knife handle. At Scout camp we swam in the mucky and slimy Clinton River and marched in and out of its swamps, which were filled with stinging itch weed.

When I got terrible acne, my mother counseled me that my pimples would rough up my skin so I wouldn't look like a girl. Eventually the acne—that horrible white ooze from inside me—subsided. I started to date. I took showers, wanted stylish clothes, and wore white bucks one year and black and white saddle shoes the next. My mother no longer had to worry about me. After a bout with Ds, I decided I would go to college and be a good student. I would be bright and sparkle like my mom and dad and the house I came from. Mom had gotten a dirty rascal off her hands.

I thank my mother not just for all the dust she cleaned but for the stories that helped me understand how my family and I, like contemporary people everywhere, have had a changing relationship with dust. She helped me compare my youth to my life forty years later on the black earth prairie of southwestern Minnesota, where my wife, Cathy, and I have lived for thirty years and raised four children.

Here winds of maritime strength blow year in and year out. They glean the countryside's particles of plant, grain, and soil. They make the spring air pulsate with pollen, fill fall days with harvest dust, turn winter's snow black, and darken the sky itself when they blow hardest. They fill the towns with bits and pieces of the surrounding countryside, and as my wife knows far better than I do, they keep our house and garage in constant need of sweeping.

Dust does not respect our family room of glass and white walls. It gathers, in the form of ash, on the stone floor of the fireplace. It collects on the mantel and diminishes, however slightly, the brightness of the airbrush painting that hangs above it. Dust gathers on the computer screen, on shelves, and on books, which themselves emit molds that make archives dangerous places for allergy sufferers. At least twice a year I set up a tall ladder to clean the skylight, whose filmy surface reminds me how light itself can be darkened by dust, how even in this age of cosmic and radioactive dusts, when supercolliders whirl in search of particles infinitely smaller than any Democritus and Lucretius imagined, dust still remains the everyday boundary between the visible and the invisible.

. . .

Aside from my mother, who told me so much about dust in her life and that of our family, my first thanks go to Eugen Weber—professor, writer, and friend. Eugen, who has taught me much over many years, helped me in several ways to write this book. Originally he sent me to the person who first recommended the topic of dust. Then he invited me to his wonderful two-day retirement party at UCLA, where I presented an early draft of what is now chapter 3 and received some useful suggestions and, more valuable, enthusiasm for my topic and approach. Later, Eugen critically read an early draft and encouraged me to clarify the book's goal in its introduction and title.

Second, I am indebted to Guy Thuillier, an immensely inventive regional historian, professor and director at the École Pratique des Hautes Études, and an officer of France's Cour des Comptes (auditor general), who should be better known in the English-speaking world by practicing historians. In the middle of a conversation at a small Parisian restaurant, he declared, "There should be a history of dust." Months later he generously furnished me with a handwritten outline of themes he would place in a history of dust.

I also thank friend and historian Jeffrey Russell, who critically read the entire manuscript, offering many valuable suggestions, none as intriguing as the notion that the confidence of contemporary Western civilization might be based on its control over small and invisible things. He then graciously agreed to write the foreword.

Special gratitude is owed to friend, colleague, and poet Phil Dacey, who helped me with the introduction, and friend, colleague, and writer David Pichaske, who improved the manuscript at many points and encouraged me to keep the preceding recollections of my mother. Life-long friend Ted Radzilowski called my attention to the place of light in cleaning up the small.

Emeritus professor Dale Sparling and professors Laren Barker and Robert Elaison, respectively of the university's earth science, biology, and chemistry programs, offered valuable advice on scientific aspects of the manuscript. Professor David Wright of Michigan State University sharpened my understanding of how twentieth-century technology extended the sight and reach of human eye and hand into the minuscule and led me to two worthwhile books on the connection between contemporary medicine and technology.

Evelyn Ostlie did research on dust in rural Minnesota for me. Donata DeBruyckere, who seems to get ensnared in most things I do, carried out a variety of research projects for me. John Radzilowski and Marianne Zarzana improved an early draft of chapter 4, and Julie Bach, always of good spirit, encouraging manner, and keen wit, went through the entire manuscript rounding off rough edges. Rhonda Fedde, a student worker in university word processing, spared me much drudgery with her faithful and accurate work.

In addition to the gratitude owed those I have named, during five years of stray conversations I have accumulated a considerable debt to others whose names I never knew or soon forgot. The declaration that I was writing a book on dust sprinkled many conversations with interesting anecdotes. At a reunion of my wife's family, one man described what happened to cars left out after a gentle rain in his hometown, which was shadowed by the smokestacks of a cement factory. After a public lecture at a nearby town in southwestern Minnesota, I heard what it is like to live beneath a constant shower of red flakes from the town's corn processing company. In a bar at the Royal Saint David's in Wales, a fellow golfer told my son and me that leather factories explode as a consequence of the concentration of fine dusts. I heard more stories about the dust storms of the 1930s than I care to recount.

My gratitude reaches from individuals, named and unnamed, to institutions and their librarians. Minitex, the interlibrary loan system of our university and the state of Minnesota, proved indispensable. Its cheery local and efficient representative, Nancy De Roode, made my quests for distant books a pleasurable treasure hunt. University reference librarians Mary Jane Striegel, Jim Kapoun, and others on the staff helped me with my searches and aided me in other ways.

The University of Minnesota library system again proved to be my second home library. I made ample use of its main library, the Wilson Library; its science and engineering library, the Walter Library; and its agricultural and medical libraries. I also spent profitable time at the Wangenstein Historical Library of Biology and Medicine. I found further valuable material at the Minnesota Historical Society, the Minnesota State Law Library, the main branch of the Minneapolis Central Library (especially its unique photographic and image collection), the St. Paul Main Library, and St. Paul's James J. Hill Reference Library.

On every front the University of California Press wins my special thanks. Executive editor Howard Boyer enthusiastically welcomed the manuscript into the Press and imaginatively and energetically supported it thereafter. He selected the book's illustrator, Abigail Rorer, and its designer, Nicole Hayward. Their work speaks for itself. In turn, without implicating them in my errors and confusions, press editors Dore Brown and Erika Büky immensely improved the book by their keen care for its development.

Finally done thanking others, I again offer my thanks to my wife, Cathy. She has abided my habit of book writing even though it voraciously consumes time and affection that could be dedicated to other things. Nurse and mother of four children, she has been attuned to the subject of this book from beginning to end. As I was writing these very acknowledgments, she called my attention to a pictorial guide to the history of Western costumes and a newspaper article on the New York American History Museum's recent exhibition on disease. In the latter I read about the haunting hantavirus. After it mysteriously killed five people in the Southwest in 1993, researchers showed that it was contracted by inhaling dust contaminated by mouse saliva, droppings, and urine. In the book on costumes, I was delighted to read about the chopine (or what the Italians called the *zocollo*). With a sole twenty-four inches thick, it was a clog-like shoe into which was slipped the elegant footwear of the sixteenth and seventeenth century. It allowed the wearer to rise above the mud and filth of the streets.

In similar fashion, I hope this book allows its reader to stand beyond the dust and dirt of everyday life and to understand how much our lives are influenced by our changing relationship to small and minuscule things. I have tried to tell a story of dust that provides a first and elementary history of the small and the invisible and suggests the possibilities of the expanding microcosm before us.

TEXT	11.5/16.5 Fournier
DISPLAY	Scala
DESIGN	Nicole Hayward
COMPOSITION	Binghamton Valley Composition, Inc.
PRINTING AND BINDING	Haddon Craftsmen, Inc.